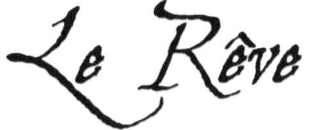

# Le Rêve

## R P WARD

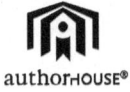

authorHOUSE®

*AuthorHouse™*
*1663 Liberty Drive*
*Bloomington, IN 47403*
*www.authorhouse.com*
*Phone: 1-800-839-8640*

*Illustrations by RP Ward*

*First published by AuthorHouse 8/15/2011*

*ISBN: 978-1-4634-1365-1 (hc)*
*ISBN: 978-1-4634-1367-5 (e)*
*ISBN: 978-1-4634-1366-8 (sc)*

*Library of Congress Control Number: 2011909766*

*Printed in the United States of America*

*Any people depicted in stock imagery provided by Thinkstock are models, and such images are being used for illustrative purposes only.*
*Certain stock imagery © Thinkstock.*

*This book is printed on acid-free paper.*

*For Cindy*

# Acknowledgments

Thank you to Suzanne Pierce-Zapata for her quiet patience and fruitful suggestions, and to Julie Calvin and Cassandra Hansen for their ongoing encouragement.

A special thank you to Mr. Cooper Edens for his thoughtful advice. Thank you to Jasmine Isperi, who read and put up with me, and to my daughter Caroline, who inspired the story, and to Leisa Smith, who challenged me to finish it. Thank you to my wife, Cindy, who gave me the space, time, and encouragement to be creative. I would also like to acknowledge John and Claude for their ongoing inspiration; they will forever be with us in spirit. Thanks to the folks at AuthorHouse. And thank you to all the children great and small; without them, this story would not have been written.

Finally, I would like to (with great love and respect) acknowledge that creative energy that lies within us all and is, without a doubt, the inspiration to all things great and small.

SGMKJ

# Introduction

When she was very young, my daughter was given the gift of a little stuffed animal. He was a well-mannered, rather handsome critter—pearly white with a rainbow horn. Caroline loved the little fellow, and it wasn't long before the three of us were fast friends.

While I'm sure many parents have communicated with their kids by talking to them with toys, I couldn't have dreamed how much fun it would be pretending to be the voice of that fuzzy little fellow! And so the story began; it wasn't until many years later that the story unfolded further.

So far, life for Caroline had been an ongoing adventure—perhaps a little like the story she and her friend Uni inspired those years ago.

In the tale a young girl, after dreaming of far-off places and all the possibilities they hold, must undergo an arduous journey, confronting her own fear and doubt while in the process of learning more about herself and "the special magic of the human spirit" that lies within.

Joseph Campbell used to say myths come from the same place dreams come from. But, because they're more linear, they're more instructive. A myth, he says, is a song of the universe—a song that, if accurately perceived, explains the universe and our oftentimes confusing place in it.

I'm inclined to believe that this yarn, this "dream-tale," is both a fairy tale and a myth. Campbell says the two are kindred. If he says myths are songs of the universe, I would hope this tale might just be a simple melody.

# The Rainbow Stone

Through the ages, from secret doctrines to ancient myths, from the open forums of ancient Athens to the secret meetings of medieval Merlin, all philosophies have made reference to a "magic stone"; a sorcerer's stone, a gem so remarkable it has been said to contain the secrets of the universe.

The sages of India sang its praises; Greek philosophers spoke of its brilliance. Today, modern-day mystics continue the search for this elusive jewel, "The Rainbow Stone" is such a gem.

# PROLOGUE

It was a dark and stormy night; the summer gale had come as a complete surprise, but there could be no turning back now. Thunder rumbled in the distance as lighting flashed against the dark, cloudy sky. In the bright light, Alicia caught a glimpse of the farmhouse. Once there, she would be able to take shelter and, with a little luck, find the girl.

The elders had warned her to be careful; there would be danger in the night. She was to find the youngster, make sure she was safe, and return to the garden. The longer she lingered, the greater the risk. Determined, she pressed on against the storm.

## Le Rêve

The young girl lay feverish; she had been delirious for nearly two days. As her father placed another cool cloth on his daughter's forehead, he worried for the youngster. He had done all he could; now he would have to help her fight the fever.

"Here's clean water, Monsieur Fairchild," a young man spoke, entering the shed.

"Thank you, Philippe; put it here," the man told him motioning, to the bed stand.

"How is she?" the youth asked.

"It's hard to say. I'll feel better when her fever lifts," he said. "Claude should be here with the doctor soon."

The youngster had been in and out of consciousness, and now, as her father felt her forehead, his eye was drawn to the little stuffed animal she cradled in her arms.

"You've been with her a long time, little fellow," he spoke in a quiet voice. "I'll never forget the day you arrived."

Feeling the weight of the long day, the man leaned back with a sigh and closed his eyes. *I'll never forget that day,* he thought drifting off. *Never …*

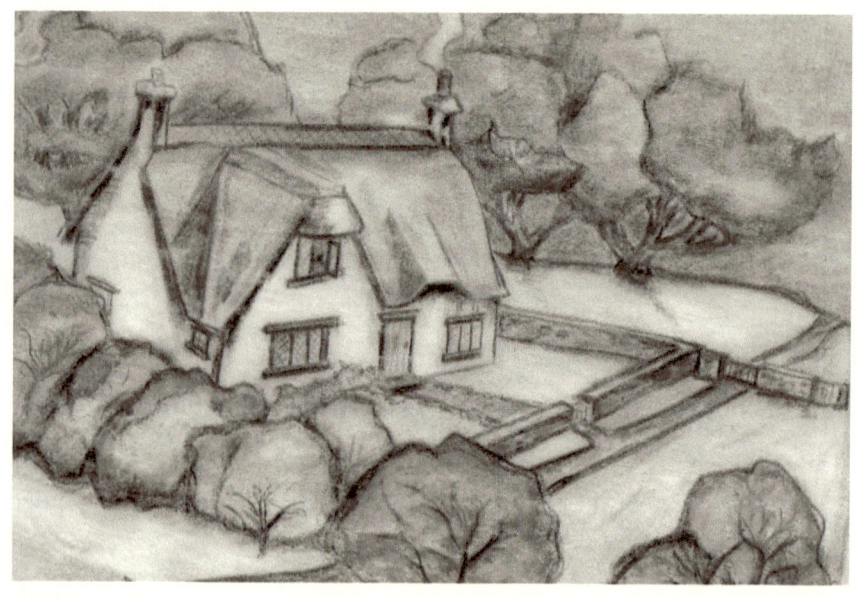

## CHAPTER I

# A Unique Friend

In truth, the little girl might have fallen instantly in love with the little fuzz head, were it not for the rather "odd thing" stuck on his nose. It was singular of nature, not large and, as best anyone could tell, of absolutely no use or consequence. Fortunately in the end it was a flaw that was easy enough to overlook, and in time forget about altogether.

Others on the farm couldn't help but make snide comments about the newcomer and his funny nose. The pig, for instance, under his breath of course, asked, "Hello, has anyone noticed that the rather odd little fellow has something looking very much like a banana stuck to his nose?"

Meanwhile, the goat, in his own inimitable fashion, was quick to point out how unusual it was to see such a noticeably needless noodle stuck atop such a notably nonsensical noggin.

In no time at all, it had become perfectly clear, to the pig and goat at least, that the newcomer, without question—yes, without a doubt—was, purely and plainly stated, a bit of an "odd duck," though, in truth, he wasn't a duck at all! This "odd duck" was, by the way, as far as they were concerned, not to be trusted! The little girl's mother, on the other hand, found her daughter's new friend to be quite charming, often remarking how sweet he actually was. By her estimation, the little fur-ball was "wonderfully unusual," and, as she so often mentioned, so very ... ah ... so very unique. Because, from the start, the word unique was so difficult for the little girl to say, her new friend would soon become known as Uni.

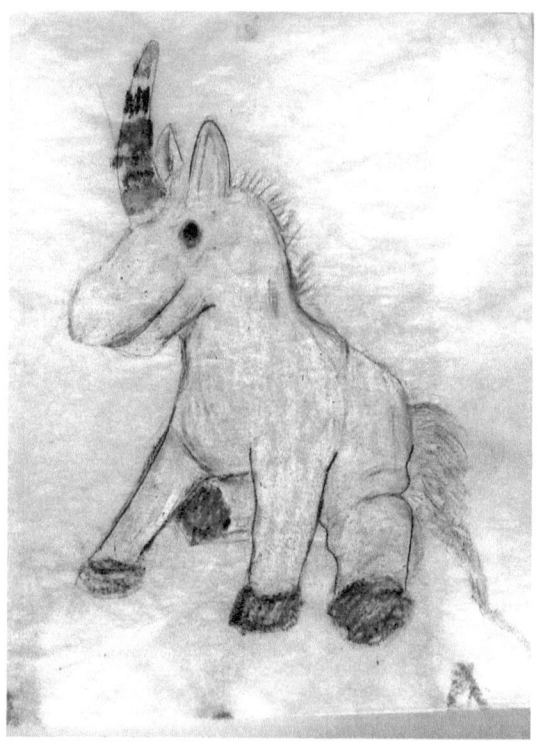

It was sometime later, after her mother had grown so very ill, that the youngster was so very grateful to have Uni by her side.

"You must live your life with love, my little one," her mother counseled, "and love the life you live."

"I will keep you in my heart and in my dreams forever," the young girl whispered with tear-filled eyes. And while the thought seemed to buoy her spirits somewhat, in her heart, there remained a deep sadness.

Following her mother's passing, life at Morning Cloud wasn't the same. Though her father was kind, he too had been deeply saddened by the loss of his wife, when, as any young girl might, his daughter complained of their hardship, her father's reply was always the same. "Remember what your mother would say: 'Little one, Count your blessings and think of those less fortunate.'" While she knew in her heart her mother's words were true, the youngster could find no comfort in them.

A few years later, her father remarried in an attempt to restore harmony to family and to Morning Cloud. Her new stepmother was a stern woman, tall and lean, with sad eyes. As it was soon discovered, she was a woman with her own ideas. In her way of thinking, there was no longer enough room in the tiny house, and so it was decided, over her father's protests, the daughter would be moved to the woodshed.

"The girl will be comfortable there!" the stepmother insisted. And so a feather bed was placed beneath the shed's small window.

## CHAPTER 2

# A Flickering Light

Some years later, as Caroline lay staring at the full moon through the shed's summer window, she thought about her mother and dreamed of life beyond the farm. The flickering candle cast dancing shadows on the rafters and tantalized her imagination. She saw gentlemen in their finery and fair maidens in their soft, satin gowns twirling round and round, and she heard the music wafting on the warm night air. Suddenly, the candle flickered in the soft summer breeze, and her so-real vision began to fade.

"Wouldn't it be wonderful, Uni?" she asked her friend with inquiring eyes. "Wouldn't it?" In his silence—to Caroline at least—her old friend seemed to agree.

Later, that night, Caroline was awakened by another flickering light. She wondered for just an instant what it could be before drifting quietly off to sleep again.

And so the flickering light may have forever remained a mystery— were it not for the wonder of dreams and all the possibilities it held.

Later that night, the light flickered again, and this time, when Caroline opened her eyes, she wasn't sure if she were awake—or only dreaming she was awake?

"Well now," a voice giggled. "It could be ya jewst might be wide awake 'n' dream'n."

"What!" Caroline cried, sitting up with a start. "Who … ah …

where … ah … who are you?" she asked with a shiver, holding Uni tight.

"I holly luv ta play hide 'n' seek with me moon shadow," the voice replied. "Hav ya tried it?"

"Who are you?" Caroline asked, gaining courage.

"Well now, lass, ain't it jewst the wit," the voice spoke. "I'd be right here in front ta ya, can't ya see me?"

"Here?" Caroline asked, reaching out toward the candle. "Careful, lass!" the voice pleaded.

In that moment, a tiny young woman with flowing red hair wearing a brief corn-silk dress, a bright blue shawl, and sequined slippers appeared next to her on the nightstand. To add to the mystery of the moment, she appeared to have a gentle glow about her.

"Oh, surry," she giggled. "I furgot, tiz a dream. I can be show'n when you're dream'n, I nary shude be otherwise!" she told Caroline with a sheepish grin.

"Otherwise?" Caroline asked.

"When yude be waken!" she replied.

"Oh, I see," Caroline said with a puzzled look on her face.

"When yude bin waken, iz pretty fare ta dream'n," the tiny miss explained. "Oary Begory! I sezs, are you dream'n or waken? Or are ya awake 'n' think'n yur dream'n? Makes me dizzy jewst try'n to keep it straight," she confessed.

The little woman asked again, "Had ya ever played hide 'n' seek with yur moon shadow?"

"Well … no … not really," Caroline admitted, feeling a little sorry that she hadn't.

"Jump'n McCevers thad ud be the fune of it!" she admitted. "And some nights can be just plain scary," she added with a shiver.

"Scary?" Caroline asked.

"O'course! That adds to the fune!" she went on.

"Depend'n on who might be snoop'n round in the dark!"

"Snoop'n round," Caroline repeated.

"It's usually after midnight when they come creep'n." she told her with another shiver.

"Midnight," Caroline echoed.

"By the saints," the tiny girl protested, by now getting a bit irritated by the constant interruptions. "Why is it you keep repeat'n me, lass?" she asked. "If I wud be need'n ta hear meself twice, I wud be say'n it 'duble' … but as luk wud hav it I, sure as day, wud be hear'n me self the first time round!"

"Is it true are there really such a thing as ghosts and goblins?" Caroline asked her.

As if she were pondering the question, her little guest hesitated for a moment before speaking. "Well now, lass, the truth known, a bunch o them scary thins can cume creep'n round … I'd be mean'n really!"''

"What?" Caroline asked with a start.

"There ya go again, want'n me to repeat meself!" she complained. "By good Saint Pat, you shude nary worry, girl. You'd be safe and sound right here in yur bed," she assured her.

"Wait a minute!" Caroline interrupted, looking at the tiny girl with curious eyes. "Who and, if you don't mind me asking, what are you?"

"Well, lass, You'll jewst have ta be the judge o that." She explained, "You cude say I'm this, you cude say I'm that. But the truth known: it's yur dream and yur imagination"

"Life tizn't always logical, young one, and dreams for sure have their own way!" She went on, "But, as they say, I'd be off the wagon!"

"I think you mean off the subject." Caroline told her "Who did you say you are?"

With that, the little lady hesitated before taking a step closer to Caroline.

"I, me young friend—and I hope you'll soon consider me as suche—am Alicia of the Briar Moore Garden, at yur service," she said with a bow. "You, lassie, can be call'n me Ali!"

"Hello, Ali, I'm Caroline," she said, introducing herself. "I really don't have many friends out here in the country," she admitted.

"Don't be forgett'n yur mum and dad and all the critters here at Morning Cloud," Ali reminded her.

"Oh, sure, I love the animals and my father and ... well ... my father has been different since my mother died," Caroline explained. "So you know my family and the farm?"

"I shude say, lass ... turns out, I'd be know'n the likes 'o' you 'n' yurs long afur yude be know'n the likes 'o' me 'n' mine!" Ali spoke.

"So you've been here a long time?" Caroline asked.

"Ya cude say that," Ali said with a wry grin. "The truth, Caroline a Morn'n Cloud," she continued. "Time iz jewst a made up, to fare it all!"

"Pardon?" Caroline asked with puzzled look on her face.

"Time is jewst a made upe!" Ali repeated.

"Made upe?" Caroline echoed.

"A made upe!" she insisted. "When ya think about it," Ali began, "There's yesterday, tomorrow, the future, and the past, but when it's all been said and done, you're still right here at last. There's sometime, most the time, and any time ... ta call ... but when it's all been said and done there's no time left at all. "The truth o it, Caroline a Morn'n Cloud," Ali spoke, standing up straight and tall in order to look as important as possible. "Thar's only now ... right now!"

"Right now," Caroline repeated, not knowing for sure what Ali was trying to tell her.

"That's it, the truth known!" she spoke, smiling at her puzzled pupil. "Now ... right now! When you fale, it you'll know! The fune a liv'n now," Ali told her, "that's when ya wud be fale'n it!"

"Fale'n it?" Caroline asked, looking puzzled.

"Fale'n the magic!" Ali spouted with a grin.      ·

"The magic," Caroline mouthed.

"The rainbow magic," Alicia added, obviously excited about the present topic. "And when you 'fale it,' the magic; I mean really 'fale it,' tiz when ya'll know!"

"Know?" Caroline asked.

"Exactly," Ali chimed in with enthusiasm. "Aye, lass, ya'll be know'n the magic, and fale'n the joy!"

"Oh!" Caroline said with a smile, finally understanding what Ali had been trying to tell her. "Feel it," she said out loud. "When you 'feel it,' you'll know!"

"Aye, lass; fale it," Ali agreed. "You'll be know'n the magic and fale'n the joy," she said with a laugh. "Ta the joy! I have to tell ya, lass," she spoke "yur wee Uni is a fine one ta be hav'n the magic, and then some."

"Uni?" Caroline repeated with a laugh. "But he's just a stuffed toy."

"Thar ya go, lass," Ali spoke. "What tiz can be a sham, giv'n the look but nary the feel," she counseled, "The truth a it, young one, is yur wee friend wud be know'n the magic and then some."

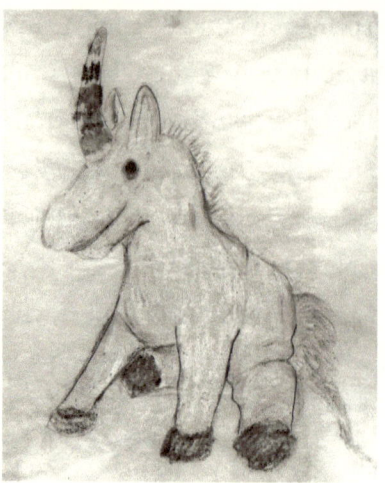

With that, Caroline picked up Uni, looking at him carefully, and in that moment, he had never seemed so alive, as if he would say or do something any minute. According to Ali, though he had been a very quiet friend, Uni had been alive all along. Caroline wasn't convinced; that would have to come later—if there was going to be a later, since, according to Ali, there was only now … right now.

Caroline sat quietly, pondering for a minute before she spoke. "The Rainbow magic," she mouthed in a quiet voice. "I bet it would be 'fune' ta play hide and seek with your moon shadow, don't you think Uni?" she asked her pal with curious eyes, wondering. In his silence, to Caroline at least, Uni all of a sudden seemed to agree.

"I'd best be go'n now," Ali spoke.

"Will you come back?" Caroline asked.

"Aye, lass, I'm forever flit'n about like a firefly in luv. Anytime yude be dream'n tiz the time I jewst might be beam'n!" she chuckled. "But before I go there's something I'd best be shar'n,"

With that Ali reached into her shoulder pouch and with drew a small, round stone. It was a silky smooth, well-polished gem appearing to sparkle of its own accord.

"This ud be a very special stone, priceless on all occasions," Ali told her. "Itud be of the magic and all its colors. If ya find truble brew'n, rub the stone, it'll put the fear in a banshee, it will!" she counseled. "It's called a Rainbow Stone," she explained, "it's just a rub ta think such a tiny thing can be hold'n so many secrets. Nary forget, young one!" Ali warned. "Use it wisely, and keep it safe."

With that she leaned and rubbed the stone with a gentle motion. At first there was nothing. But then, from deep within the stone, came a shimmering blue light. Caroline could only watch as the light began expanding, growing bigger and bigger, filling up the room before bursting into millions of tiny sparkling jewels of rainbow color!

At first, Caroline was dazzled by the colorful light show, but her beguile was short-lived when she noticed she had lost Ali.

"Ali, where are you?" Caroline cried.

"Well now, lass, I'd be right here, in the thick o things!" her tiny friend giggled. "Ain't it jewst the glory?"

As Caroline looked closer, to her relief, she found her friend perched a top the nightstand, shimmering bright with all the colors.

"Ali!" Caroline cried, "are you alright?!"

And in that next instant, the millions of shimmering jewels were sucked back into the stone with a "whoosh."

"Now ain't it jewst the glory!" Ali cried.

"I was afraid I'd lost you!" Caroline confessed.

"Don't be afraid, girl!" Ali encouraged, "be 'fale'n the joy!

"Begory!" Ali cried as she spied the morning light creeping through shed's small window. "Tiz the time fur sleep'n girl, you shude be turn'n round ta the land of dreams" she said whispering in Caroline's ear. "May yur sleep'n be still, yur dreams be sweet, 'n' may ya be safe and sound till next we meet."

Instantly Caroline's lids grew heavy, and, as if she were caught in a spell, she was soon fast asleep.

"Next time, we'll be gett'n ta know yer moon shadow!" Ali promised. "Ta the joy!" she whispered as she disappeared into the night!

## CHAPTER 3

# The Best Things in Life

After meeting Ali, Caroline found herself with a renewed enthusiasm for her life at Morning Cloud. When she pulled weeds in the pea patch, she stopped to smell the fragrant blossoms. When she carried hay to the barn, she delighted in the playful lambs. Tossing grain to the noisy goose, she couldn't help but laugh at the cantankerous old fellow and his hilarious honking.

Caroline had taken Ali's counsel to heart and stopped to smell the blossoms. It was so simple. As Ali suggested, "Good things are all around us if we just open our eyes," and so Caroline eagerly looked forward to her visits with her Ali.

It was during one of the visits that Caroline told Ali of her growing desire to see what the rest of the world had to offer; the world far away and beyond the little farm of Morning Cloud.

"I truly appreciate all you've taught me," Caroline told her friend, "but I know in my heart I have to go, I've got to find my own way."

"Well now, lass," Ali replied, "it's shy ta be larn'n girl, but tiz clear as day the wanderlust has cume calling," she told her. "Hear'n ya, wud be remind'n me of a lad I once knew:" she began; "He was a fine lad, a shepherd boy liv'n with his grandpa high upe in a lovely mountain meadow. Thar was a time the lad truly luved mind'n a bonney bunch 'o' sheep being all wooly 'n' the like, but one day, it cum ta fare out to the lad that tend'n sheep was none better than watch'n paint dry on a rainy day.

"Well now, as it turns out the lad's grandpa wud be know'n the boy like the back of his hand and would be tell'n him a old-timer stury ta be sett'n him straight.

"'Now hear me lad,' the old man told the boy, 'since ya got the urge to be a travl'n man, I best be tell'n ya about a sight for sav'n special. Ta stops ya in your tracks, like a tiger in the tar pits!

"'As legend would have it … way off yonder way beyond them high-top mountains, in a green green valley far, far away, there'd be a village—an enchanted village at that—a downright tinsel-town delight be'n all made upe, all made upe believe it or not, all made upe a gold.

"'Begory,' his grandpa went on, "it was many years ago now. I'd been search'n some three days gone for a little lost lamb when it first caught me eye,' he told the lad. 'by the saints, I says, it can't be! But there it was: an enchanted town all right, and all shimmer'n and shin'n, all made upe a that shin'n yellow metal—all made upe a gold.

"'Now listen, boy,' his grandpa said, 'Ta find that tinsel town, ya must be go'n way over yonder to the high-top mountain and way down through the deep green valley some three days gone, and in the early morn'n hour, be wait'n. When the morn'n sun is on the rise, tiz when you wud be see'n it—right then there, just shin'n bright,' His grandpa told him. 'And when ya see it is when you'll know … you'll be know'n right where the treasure lies.

"'There'd be a poem, lad,' The old man told the boy:

The city 'o' gold
The stories told
Is of the stuff 'o' dreams
The riches thar may vanish 'n' air

Be'n nary what they seem
A shin'n star that finds it,
Will guide ya all the way
Ta find the mystery 'n' the magic
Of that shine'n brand new day!


"Well now, the youngster wuz jewst jump'n to be hear'n his grandpa's stury, decid'n right then 'n' there, as sure as the moon, to be head'n ta that high-top mountain. When he'd be see'n that shin'n light, he'd be a travl'n man the likes a one, two, three—travel'n straight 'n' true ta that tingle-topped tinsel town, all made upe a that shimmer'n 'n' shin'n metal—all made upe a gold!

"'For sure there has ta be treasure wait'n!' the boy told his grandpa. 'For sure there has ta be treasure!'

"Well now lass, tiz late!" Ali told Caroline, changing the mood of the evening. "We best be finish'n the stury next time!"

"No!" Caroline protested. "You can't stop now, you've got to tell me: did he find it? Did he find the city of gold?"

"Begory, lass, tiz time for sleep'n," Ali spoke with a wave of her hand. "The stury can wait!"

"That's not fair," Caroline groaned, already yawning. Soon she was fast asleep.

## CHAPTER 4

# *Into the Night*

An eerie silence hung on the cold night air as Ali made ready to return to the garden. She had stayed late, and now, as she turned to go, a chill ran down her spine.

She knew all too well the longer she waited, the greater the danger. At times she'd heard noises or felt something or someone watching her from the shadows. She'd been scolded by the elders for staying late—for being foolish.

"Saints, help us, will ya shy be learn'n, girl?" the gatekeeper had warned "Beware the night thins! They'll be stale'n yur heart and yur dreams. A tiny miss the likes 'o' you shud be safe 'n' sound in the briar long afore them game'n creatures come call'n!"

"Stale yur heart and stale yur drems," Ali spoke out loud. "Aye it's the nod, sure as rain, I won't be show'n, and they won't be know'n!" She thought as she moved toward the window, *May the sun go fad'n if they think they'll be stale'n the likes a me 'n' mine! One day I will be travel'n further than the briar,* she thought. *That'll be the day; that'll be the day fur sure.*

"Ta the joy, Uni," Ali whispered moving toward the window. "I'll see ya in yur dreams." In his silence, Uni seemed to agree. Ali rubbed the stone, knowing she would soon be back in the briar. Sure it was late, but what harm was done? She always loved this time; being carried home by the magic. It was a tingling feeling, like becoming light itself.

17

*I'd be of the be'n the magic, and the be'n the magic is of me,* she thought as she made ready to return to the garden. As the familiar sensation began, every molecule in her body danced the familiar tune. But suddenly, something was horribly wrong. It was a strange feeling—a dizzy feeling. She was weak, very weak—struggling to stay upright, to stand up. *The night thins,* she thought, her head spinning. In that next moment she heard a creepy voice calling.

## The Stranger in the Night

"Is that you, my dear?" the voice called from the darkness. "At last, I've found you."

Struggling to clear her head, Ali was startled as a hooded figure materialized from the shadows and moved toward her. As the figure approached she could just make out a cloaked woman's face in the pale moonlight, with its sunken eyes and crooked nose nearly touching her thin lips.

As the woman approached, she spoke with a salacious grin. "I can show you the way," she promised. "Come with me and have it all: wealth and power beyond your wildest dreams!"

"Who are you?" Ali asked, still struggling to clear her head.

"You know me, my dear," the pale woman assured her with a sinister smile. "I've always been with you."

"You!" Ali spoke, summoning her courage. "I don't know you.

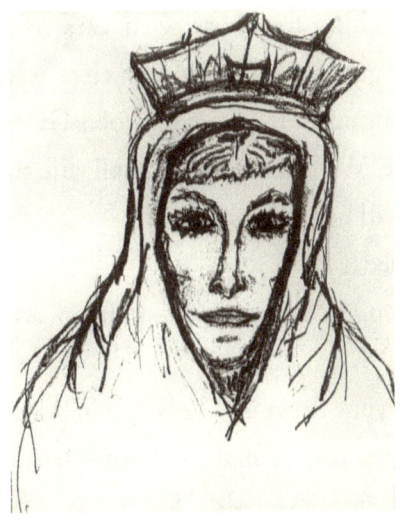

"Oh, but you do!" the woman insisted. "When you've been angry, when you've seen fit to defy the elders, when you have been outraged, jealous, or ashamed, I've been there in the shadows standing by you. I am of the shadows and the night!" She cackled, "I am your savior, your confident—join me and have it all!"

Ali was dumfounded! So, it was true, they would try to steal your heart and your dreams! "But I'd be jewst a wee lass from the garden," Ali pleaded. "What wud ya be want'n with the likes 'o' me 'n' mine?"

"Yes, my dear, I am well aware of who you are," she spoke, her beady eyes fixed on Ali's. "It's true you are indeed a simple garden girl." The woman smirked. "But there is one thing you have that I do not: one thing I must possess ... sssss ..." she hissed "The magic—the secrets of the magic!"

"But the magic is in everything!" Ali told her.

"Of course, my dear, I'm sure it is!" the woman marveled. "And you will help me find it."

"But you wud be of the magic!" Ali told the cloaked woman. "What's the point 'o' find'n what ya wud be hav'n?"

19

"Save your preaching for those with ears to listen!" the woman snapped. "You will give me the magic or else!" Oddly, her tone then softened. "You see, my dear," the woman cooed, "It is in your best interest to give me the magic. With the magic, I shall rule the night forever, and your young friend will be safe in her bed!"

"What?" Ali cried.

"A stolen dream, a nightmare remains …sssssss!" the woman cackled.

"They will steal your dreams …" echoed in Ali's head.

"It would be very unfortunate for your friend to suffer horrific visions!" the hooded figure warned. "Why is it, do you think, so many have been locked away? They beg, they plead!" she spoke with feigned concern. "They say the nightmares are so real, but no one listens, and then they're locked up, and it's away with the key!" she cackled again with fiendish delight.

"No!" Alicia pleaded. "Leave her be!" she begged. "I'd be travl'n with ya if yude be leav'n the yung one safe in her bed with jewst her dreams 'n' noth'n more!" she bargained.

"Of coarse … sssss my dear!" the woman hissed. "Of course."

"Very well," Ali replied "On yur promise."

"The Queen of Darkness keeps her word," the woman assured her, staring into the night before turning again to face Ali. "You'll see, my dear," she spoke reassuringly. "We shall tame the magic together; there will be nothing to stop us!"

"I'd be go'n with ya," Ali told her, "but it won't be to me like'n."

"So be it," the woman snapped. "The morning light is upon us; we must hurry! We must go with the night!" she warned.

At that moment, two dark figures with an awkward gait approached from the shadows, making their way toward the shed.

"My Queen," said the first, drawing near. "All hail Drizelda!"

"All hail Drizelda!" parroted the second.

"Very well, my lord," the queen spoke impatiently. "It is my wish that you escort this one to the castle, post haste!"

"Your wish is my command, Majesty!" the first replied.

"Let her be borne of the lantern!" the queen commanded.

"The lantern?" Ali asked.

"It will be a safe and comfortable way to travel, my dear, you'll see," the woman assured her with a sinister smile.

And before she could object, the creature closest to Ali grabbed the tiny one, dropping her into the urn.

"With care, my lord!" the thin-lipped women snapped. "I hold you responsible for her safety, on your life!"

With no trace of emotion, the weasel-like creature hoisted the lantern, studying its tiny occupant for a moment before turning and heading toward the forest. The second one, clumsier than the first, stumbled as he turned, knocking a flower pot from the shed's sill.

## CHAPTER 5
# A Friend Lost, a Friend Found

The sound of the smashing pot woke Caroline from her troubled sleep, and she sat up with a start. She spotted Ali's lone slipper lying on the windowsill, its silver sequins sparkling in the moonlight.

"Ali," she whispered, standing up and peering into the night. As her eyes searched the darkness, they were drawn to a gentle glow floating on the night and moving slowly away from the shed, toward the dark wood.

*I can't let them take her; I've got to rub the stone,* she thought. But, to her dismay, she found the stone was gone! Her mind raced as she watched the distant light growing faint.

In the next instant, she heard a voice calling. "Remember the magic," it said

"Ali?" Caroline asked out loud, glancing behind her.

"And all its colors."

"Where are you?" she asked again, looking behind her.

Suddenly Caroline felt herself falling, sinking, tumbling over and over, finally landing with a thud in a cramped, smelly chamber. It was difficult to breathe, and the swaying motion made her sick—nauseous. She panicked; she had to find away out, she had to. And then, mercifully, in the blink of an eye, she was back in the shed, filling her lungs and breathing deeply, grateful to be out of that smelly, damp, dark chamber.

"Ali," Caroline whispered. "That was awful. I can't let them take her, Uni. I've got to stop them! Ali told us that, when you 'fale it,' you'll know." She told him, "I know this much: I've got to help her!" In his silence, her old friend seemed to agree.

## An Enchanted Forest

Dark clouds teased the moon as Caroline made her way deeper into the forest. Tiny creatures scurried from underfoot, and curious yellow eyes nestled in their leafy branches followed her every move as she passed. In the distance, the sound of a hoot owl drifted on the cool night air.

*I've got to keep up*, Caroline thought. *I can't lose them! I'll never see Ali again.* It was at that moment that, to her surprise, the light in the distance stopped.

Wondering, Caroline made her way toward the amber shine, placing one foot down, then shifting her weight and placing the other down, moving ever so cautiously, until she found herself close enough to make out the shapes of the two creatures standing in the pale moonlight, holding the lantern on the other side of the thicket.

"Hush!" the taller one snapped. "Did you hear that?"

"Hear what?" his partner asked.

"That!" the tall one whispered.

Caroline froze.

"I didn't hear anything!" the smallest whined.

As the closest one to her stepped into the moonlight, Caroline could just make out a weasel-like creature with beady, black-bean eyes jerking this way and that, searching the shadows.

Caroline was holding very still, barely breathing, when, to her horror she made a misstep and tumbled from her hiding place. There was an awkward silence as the startled creatures gawked at the disheveled girl on the ground in front of them.

Caroline spoke first. "Oh, ah, hi," she sputtered, jumping up and dusting herself off, acting as nonchalantly as possible.

"What is it?" the smaller of the two whimpered.

"It's just the girl from the shed," the larger one explained.

"Girl?" he whined, uncertain of her intention.

"Yes, the girl."

Caroline interrupted. "It's true: I'm a girl, but no worries," she assured him, trying to ease the tension of the moment.

As Caroline's eyes strained in the darkness, she could just make out Ali's tiny form lying on the bottom of the lantern. *I've got to keep calm,* Caroline thought. *I've got to figure a way to convince these, these mutants to release her!*

"She's just a simple garden girl, please let her go," Caroline heard herself say.

"Garden girl, that's a good one," snickered the creature holding the lantern. "This one has magic and will give it to the queen or else!" he huffed.

"Or else?" Caroline repeated.

"She'll end up like the others!" he told her.

"Others?" she wondered out loud.

"Soup," he said.

"Yes, soup!" The second said with a snicker. "Soup of the day."

"The queen believes that, by dining on her guests, she will get what they have—in this case the fairy magic," the larger of the two informed her.

"Fairy? You've made a terrible mistake. Ali is a simple garden girl." Caroline insisted.

"Mistake?" said the one holding the lantern. "The fairies have made the mistake!" He snarled, "Her majesty wants the magic, and dinner will be served!"

"I know you're mistaken," Caroline told them. "She's just a simple garden girl, and I demand that you release her!"

"Not on your life!" The one holding the lantern snarled. "By the way, if she's not a fairy, then I don't have teeth." He spoke as he moved closer to Caroline, holding up the lantern. "Look closely, girl," he insisted. "What do you see?"

As she peered through the lantern's glass, Caroline could just make out Ali's tiny form without her shawl, lying on the bottom of the urn. She guessed her eyes had to be playing tricks in the dim light, because, for an instant, she saw two tiny lacy wings lying on her friend's petite little shoulders.

"If you, ah, let her go, I, ah, ah, I … I … will protect you!" Caroline told them. "Yes, that's it! Ah … I will protect you," she said again with assurance in her voice.

With Caroline's proposal, the two creatures looked at each other, grimacing dramatically for a moment before letting out a long, lingering, belching, queasy sound.

"If that's a laugh," she told them, "this is no laughing matter."

The creature holding the lantern looked at his tiny prisoner, and then back to Caroline before speaking. "We are of the order of the Royal Dweazel, dedicated to the service of the queen and Drizland. Long live the queen!" they shouted in unison "Long live Drizelda!"

"Now be off, girl!" The larger of the two warned.

With time running short, Caroline grabbed for the lantern.

"Not on your life!" the creature snarled.

"Let … go!" Caroline demanded.

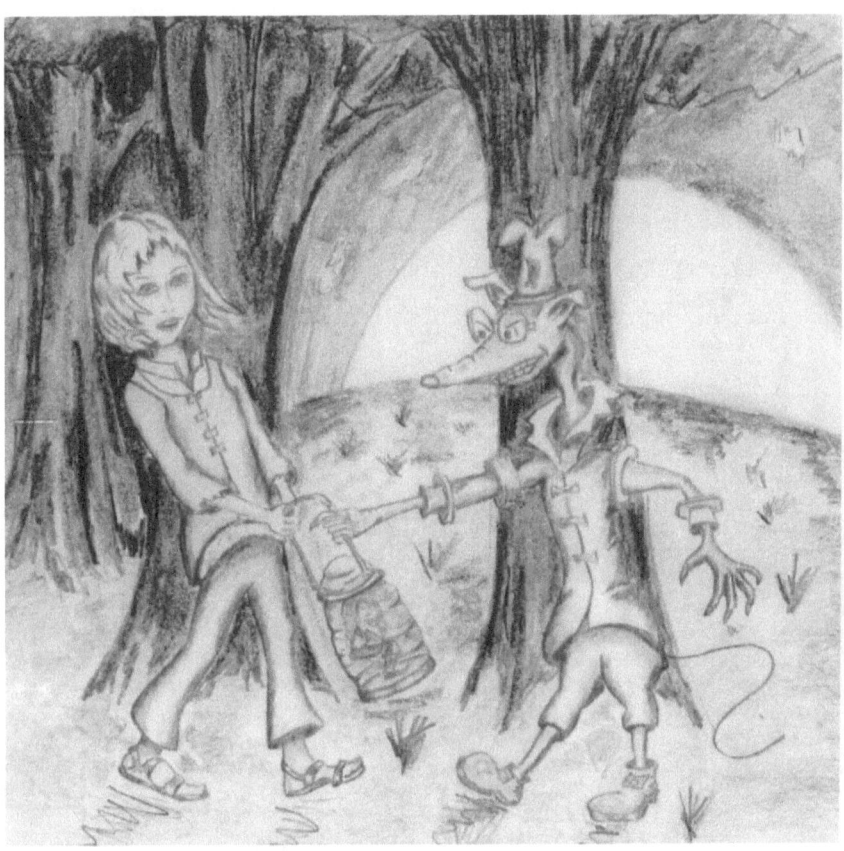

As they struggled, the full moon settling on the morning sky cast long, dark shadows that crept slowly over the open meadow.

"You can't take her!" Caroline cried.

"She belongs to the queen!" the dweazel snarled.

The tug of war had continued for some time until Caroline was distracted by a tall and particularly wobbly moon shadow teetering at the edge of the forest clearing.

"It's a ... ah ... a monster!" the dweazel shouted as he too spotted the long and tall silhouette. Whatever it was appeared to be extremely tall and quite unsteady as it began staggering toward them from the far side of the clearing.

"Oh my," Caroline said as she turned to confront the approaching apparition. "Who ... ah ... what are you?"

"It's a monster!" cried the one holding the lantern. "Run!" And with Caroline distracted, turning to meet the staggering giant, the dweazel tightened his grip on the lantern and ran off into the forest.

"Wait, you can't take her!" Caroline cried "You can't, you just can't ... wait ... come back ... Ali!"

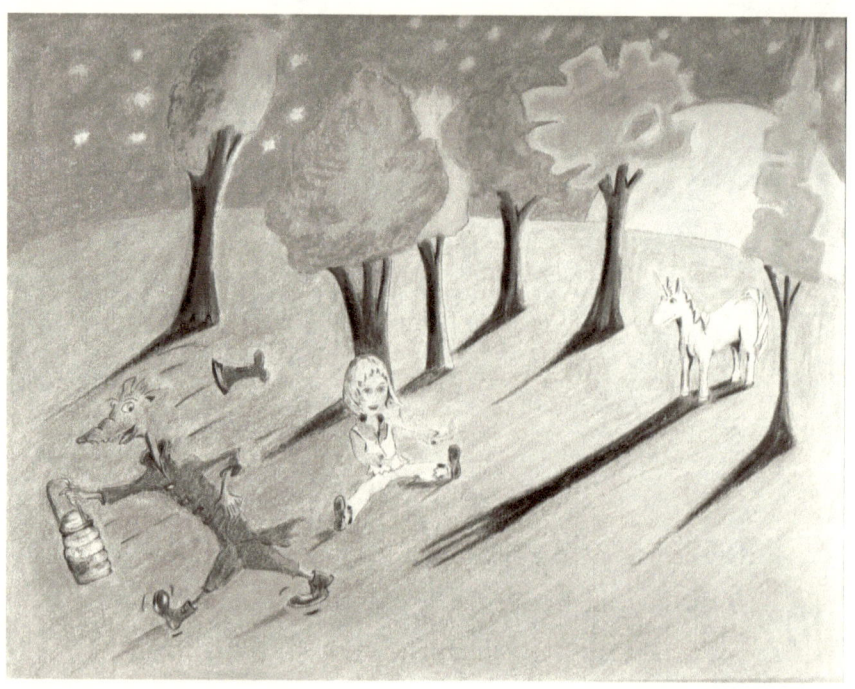

But it was too late; Ali was gone, and Caroline had a bigger problem on her hands as the staggering giant stumbled toward her. She was just getting ready to run or scream or both when, much to her surprise, she heard an oddly familiar voice wafting in her direction on the cool morning breeze.

"Caroline" the voice asked. "Is that you?"

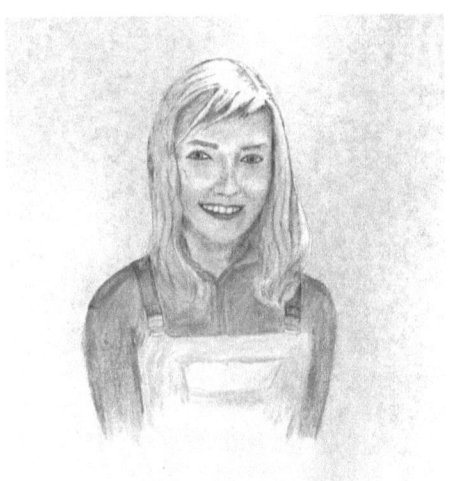

Caroline was completely taken aback. In the beginning the long moon shadow had made the thing tittering at the edge of the meadow appear extremely tall. Now, with the full moon nestled on the horizon directly behind, it was now more than obvious that the critter stumbling in her direction was, in reality, very little.

"As it turns out," Caroline informed her wobbly guest, "you're not as big as I thought. I can see now that you're really quite small."

"I'm not sure," the creature replied, obviously winded. "Am I dreaming, or is this real? I'm not sure just how I feel. One minute, I think I'm dreaming, and the next I'm awake. But if in fact I'm dreaming ... it's hard to keep it straight."

"Ali always said, there are times you just might be wide awake in a dream," Caroline told her unexpected visitor. "Uni, is that you?" Caroline asked. "I can't believe it!"

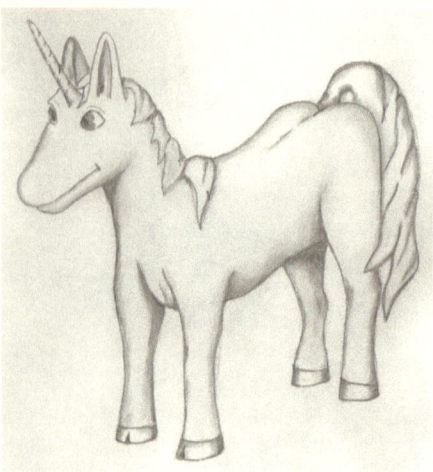

"This walking really is fun," he told her. "I think I'm getting the hang of it. It's one foot in front of the other ... one step ... two steps ... three steps, four ..."

"This is crazy!" Caroline chuckled. "Ali always told me you had the magic. I guess I refused to believe it," she admitted "It's crazy ... this is amazing!"

And so, with the full moon settling on the morning sky, the two travelers stood in the enchanted forest, reminiscing and feeling thankful that, by some crazy stroke of luck, they had managed to find each other in this rather frightening but, as they both agreed, exhilarating enchanted forest.

"After some of those days in the fields, I was so exhausted there, was absolutely no chance of dreaming," Caroline told her friend.

"That's for sure!" Uni agreed. "Hey, speaking of dream'n, have you seen Ali?" he asked. "Isn't she around here somewhere?"

"Those creatures, those mutants, the dweazels have taken her," Caroline told him, with grave concern in her voice. "And we've got to find her—find a way to get her back."

Meeting with a Mentor

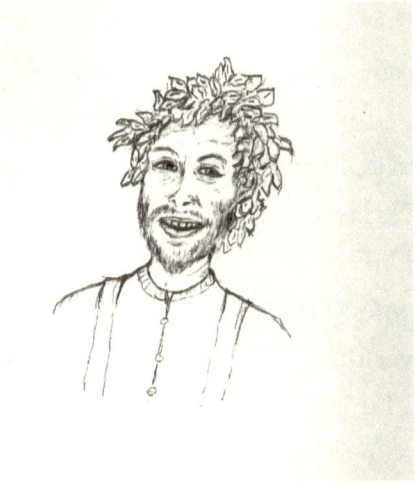

"Ahum" Uni and Caroline turned toward the sound in time to see a stranger, borne of the morning's mist, materialize next to them.

"Who are you?" Caroline asked, stepping back to get a better look at their surprise guest.

"Burble" he replied. "I am Burble," he repeated with a chuckle. He was a tall fellow, wearing a garland of leaves draped rather fashionably upon his head, a broad, toothy grin, and twinkling eyes set above his broad nose. A bright orange shirt buttoned all the way to its top hugged his slightly large belly before disappearing beneath baggy trousers held aloft by wide suspenders. On his bare feet, he wore leather sandals.

"Well then … ah … Burble," Caroline spoke with all the enthusiasm she could muster, "I'm Caroline, and this is my friend, Uni."

"Ah, a one horn," the man said nodding his approval.

"Okay, then." Caroline surmised, "I suppose it would follow, here in an enchanted forest, that you would be ah … ah … let me guess: a troll?"

"A troll!" the man groaned rolling his eyes and chuckling to himself. "Burble is not a troll … I am Burble"

31

"Yes, of course you are. I'm sure you are," Caroline returned. By now Uni appeared to be getting a bit of a laugh from the exchange.

"What do you think, Uni?" Caroline asked, turning to face her friend.

"Well," Uni said, hesitating. "I ... I really don't think he's a troll."

"Why's that?" Caroline asked, giving Uni a quirky look.

"Because," Uni spoke, lowering his voice, "I have a feeling." Whispering, he said, "I mean I'm pretty sure." He looked past her, into the trees ... "Over there," he whispered, motioning toward the thick bush. "I think ... I think ... that's a troll!"

As it stomped out of the trees, the rank smell hit them first, even before they got a full view of the heinous creature, with its vacant stare and a toothless grin. A threadbare vest hung on its hairy torso, ending ragtag just above his tattered trousers, while his tiny head appeared much too small for his large body.

"Run, Caroline!" Uni hollered as the drooling hulk stomped toward her.

"Uuh!" the troll bellowed.

"Go away!" Caroline stammered, stumbling backward as the troll stomped closer.

"Uuh!" the troll bellowed again, snatching a handful of air

"Leave her alone!" Uni shouted, charging headlong at the beast. But before he knew what hit him, a hairy arm had knocked him, head over hooves, into the bushes.

Uni was upset with himself; the troll had swatted him like a fly. Now, as the behemoth stomped toward Caroline, Uni shook himself and cleared his head.

"Uuh!" the monster belched, by now, nearly within reach of his quarry.

Uni knew he hadn't a minute to spare; he couldn't afford to

underestimate the troll this time. Lowering his head, he took a deep breath, gathering all his strength, and ran straight and true as fast as he could, right at and, this time, right into the great hulk with a thud.

"Ooooooooooh! Noooooooo! Ahhh! Noooooooo!" the troll cried. In that next instant, incredibly, as you may have guessed, the lumbering hulk was turned, right then and there, into stone. And then, remarkably, with the forest trio watching, it began melting, transforming as it did so into tiny, shimmering shards of radiant rainbow colors.

It was after this transformation was completely complete and, following a brief pause, during which the shimmering behemoth shown extremely bright, that it simply and inexplicably vanished with a poof.

Uni just stood there, not knowing for sure what to think, as silence once again befell the meadow.

"Are you all right, Caroline?" he asked.

"Thank you, Uni, thank you," Caroline, still shaking in her shoes, told her friend.

"Very good, my little quadruped," Burble spoke, "You have a big heart, my small friend."

For Everything There Is a Season

"What was that?" Caroline asked Burble with a shiver.

"All things must pass, young one," the twinkle-eyed man told her. "The troll was nothing more than your fear, you are not your fear," he explained. "You must let it go."

"The troll's gone," Uni announced. "We're safe!"

"For the time being," Burble assured them, looking at the two pilgrims with a wry grin "It appears your journey has just begun."

"Who are you?" Caroline asked.

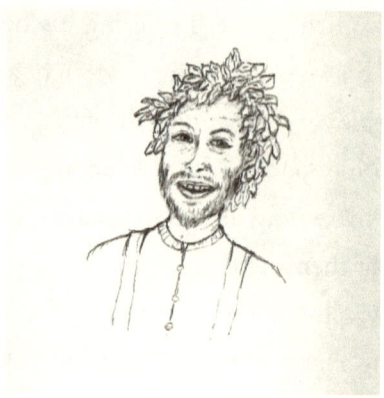

"I am Burble," he replied, "and your one-horned friend is of the magic"

"A 'one horn,'" Caroline repeated, looking at the floppy thing on her friend's nose.

"It's obvious to me now," she said. "It's odd that I couldn't see it before!"

"For everything there is a season, young one," Burble explained. "And you, young lady, are fortunate; you will need his help. to find your friend! And find her, you must. I fear she is in grave danger!" Burble hesitated for a moment, looking deep into the wood before returning his attention to his two guests. "And so this night, a journey you have begun." He told them, "You must travel to a dark land to find the light."

"May the Magic Be with You"

All was silent as the morning light crept upon the meadow.

"Which way do we go?" Caroline asked, her eyes searching the shadows.

"The Forest of Shadows," said a distant voice. "You must find the Forest of Shadows!"

"But I'm not sure we can find the way," Caroline worried.

"It's easy to doubt yourself," said a whisper on the wind

Uni took a deep breath, feeling a little stronger and perhaps just a bit wiser. Burble had warned them to be careful traveling in the deep wood. Things may not always be as they seem; a trail may lead to somewhere, or it might lead to nowhere. "Rely on yourself. Trust no one," he cautioned. "Be prepared to doubt your doubts if need be. Remember the magic and follow your heart."

## CHAPTER 6

# The Forest of Shadows

The two pilgrims made their way, single file along the narrow path winding deeper and deeper into the thick wood, with its heavy, moss-hung branches choking out the sun and allowing only a slender beam to penetrate the darkness from time to time. Soon the light from the meadow where they had entered the enchanted forest became just a bright hole in the distance behind them. The thick silence let them hear every footstep as they shuffled along, while the trees above them appeared to lean and listen as they passed. The path itself was narrow and wound in and out among the thick trunks. As their eyes grew used to the dimness, they could see only a little way on either side of the trail, where stood sordid and sinister dark shapes and shadows. Occasionally a shining shard of sunlight had the luck to slip through an opening in the canopy of leaves high above. With still a little more luck, it was not denied by the tangled limbs and matted bows waiting below, and so it pierced the darkness and shone thin and bright before them. But this became a rarity, happening less and less as they moved further into the wood.

There was no movement of air down under the forest ceiling, and it was overwhelmingly still, dark, and stuffy, bringing them to hate the forest. Even though there seemed to be even less hope of any ending, they had no choice but to go on, long after they were sick for the sight of the sun and the sky and the feel of the wind on their faces. At times, the woods became beyond so pitch dark that Caroline was barely able see her hand in front of her face.

It was then that a crystal glow suddenly appeared just beyond the borders of their vision, offering a glimmer of hope in their otherwise dark and hopeless world. It had been only a glimmer at first—a tiny sparkle in the corner of her eye that attracted Caroline's attention. She thought it her imagination, but seconds later, it splashed again with its brilliant, shimmering sparkles against the trundled tree trunks, only a stone's-throw distance, like the ocean spray in a winter's storm. They found themselves at once enamored by the spontaneous, stardust froth and its casual knack of shedding light on their otherwise dark and dreary world.

And so it was, with their spirits buoyed by their recent good fortune of the gift of the mysterious light show, they pressed on in hopes of discovering the source of this surprising splash of light—of hope. But as time passed, it was, alas, only the heavy dank darkness of the stuffy forest closing in around them that they did discover. After a time, they found themselves once again shuffling along very much as before, with heavy hearts listening and wondering about the muffled sounds of their own fallow foot steps.

"I can barely see the path ahead of me, Uni," Caroline told him. "I'm so tired and thirsty. I'm afraid I'm losing it, my friend. Do you think this can possibly be the way?" she asked him. "If only we might see the light again." But when she turned to find her friend, Caroline discovered, much to her chagrin, that he was no longer behind her. In the midst of their pending peril, he had somehow managed to up and disappear.

A Reflection of One Horn

Meanwhile, in another part of the forest, Uni, thinking Caroline was behind him, whispered over his shoulder. "I see something ahead; I can't quite make it out. It's some sort of light. There, over there; do you see it?" he asked.

A Light in the Forest

The shimmering orb hovered in the distance at first, as if hiding behind the thick, tree-trunk silhouettes made by its own accord, before seemingly shedding some shyness and drifting coyly in Uni's direction.

The white oval drifted quietly closer, its silver glow flushing imagined goblin shadows from the gnarled limbs of trees as it passed before coming to a sudden and unexpected halt, hovering mysteriously, sensing Uni's presence.

It was then, remarkably, after a brief hesitation, that the mercurial orb began transforming itself. At first it stretched into a long oval and extended, one after the other, tentacle-like limbs from its glossy surface. It then peeling away its onion layers, slowly ever so gradually revealing a very large, very white, and very glossy, well-muscled creature with a bushy mane, a flowing tail, and a rapier-like horn, singular in nature.

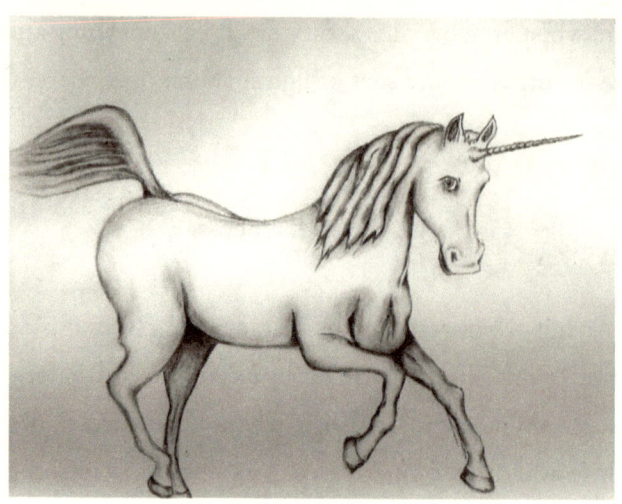

Uni was awestruck as the luminous giant galloped toward him from the shadows.

As he drew near, the Great One Horn slowed gradually before coming to a full and complete stop, standing directly in front of and towering over Uni, while looking down at him with a stern gaze.

## You Can Listen as Well as You Hear

"Hear me, young one!" the great creature spoke with a barrel-deep voice, "for you are on a journey; there is a path you must follow. You, my small friend, are of the becoming. What you are not, you must become and will become. Now, my small friend, you must take this reflection and make it yours!"

Uni was confused; he was trying to understand. Clearly the magnificent creature must be wrong; after all, he was just a little stuffed toy. What did he mean by "take this reflection"? And was he coming or going? And what could he possibly know? And how could he become anything other than what he was?

"Your misgivings are what they are," the great creature spoke. "Leave them; they are not real. It is only the magic that is real, and it is the magic that will guide you," he assured Uni. "Now, my small one you must drink from the sacred pool."

"Ah, excuse me, Your Largeness," Uni asked. "what pool would that be?"

"It would be that pool," the Great One Horn told him as a placid, dark pool appeared just steps from where the two stood.

"Oh, that pool!" Uni replied.

Remembering Burble's warning, Uni hesitated for a moment before stepping to the edge of the pond.

## The World Is as You See It

At first, as he drank, he wasn't sure he could feel it, but, soon, with his eyes wide open and fixed on his own rippling reflection, he could see it! It was hard to believe, but, as he felt the energy rushing through his body, it became more and more apparent: he was indeed growing, bigger and bigger!

All he could do now was to hang on as the ground beneath him grew more distant. His legs stretched tenfold; and he dazzled at the wondrous sights that came with his newly heightened perspective. Bigger and bigger he grew, until his previously tiny form had reached one of remarkable and unusual size. *Wow!* Uni thought. ... *Now* that *was some drink of water!*

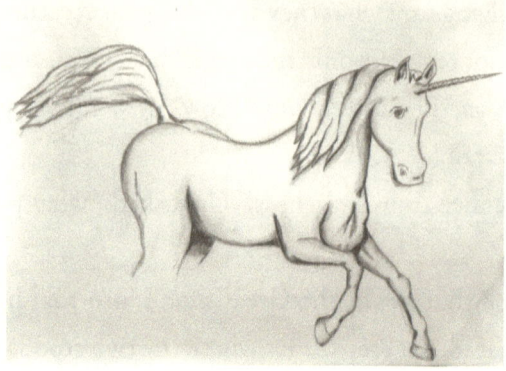

It wasn't long after he stood, adjusting and getting use to his new body size, that a voice spoke to him from the ether.

"Hear me, young one; you are now of the reflection. You must travel to a dark land to find the light."

## A Shadow of Doubt

Uni panicked as a thousand questions filled his head. *Why me? I may be bigger, but I for sure don't feel any wiser!*

"Excuse me, ah, Your Largeness, ah … I mean, Your Greatness!" He spoke, his eyes searching the shadows. "I hope you can hear me. I'm honored that you have given me, or at least loaned me such, a wonderful new, ah, shape … ah form … ah body, and I realize you expect me to use it for good and all the things you said, but I'm sorry, Your Greatness; I don't feel like I am who you think I am.

"I may look different," he continued, enjoying his newfound perspective. "I like the view from up here and all, but I don't really feel the part—I don't feel any wiser. How can I possibly make a difference?" he asked.

"Know this, young one:" the voice said reassuringly; "You are of the magic. It is the magic that will guide you."

At that moment, the Great One Horn spoke to his reluctant pupil with a sense of urgency. "It is time! You must go! Find your friend; I sense she is in grave danger." He warned, "She resides in the shadows but is not of them. She is fooled by a fool who would destroy her." He continued, "Beware: there is a witch in the wood who would want the wonders of the wizards. She is of the darkest darkness; she will steal your heart and steal your dreams. Now go! Find your friend! May the magic be with you!"

# CHAPTER 7

## *Falling*

It wasn't long after Uni had vanished that Caroline heard a voice calling. She stood quietly for a few moments, listening, but hearing only silence. A shiver ran down her spine. *I got myself into this mess*, she thought. *I could turn around and go back, but if I do, I'll never see Ali again.*

She had stayed a while, listening and calling, after being separated from Uni, but now she had a strong feeling she should keep moving. Dark shadows cast their spell as Caroline walked along the path, able to see only a few steps in front of her in the dim light. *I'll be glad to get out of this dark wood*, she was thinking when, suddenly, a wispy voice called her name.

"Caroline?" the voice echoed in the darkness. "Caroline!" the voice called again, this time louder.

"Ali?" Caroline asked.

"Caroline," the voice pleaded, "Help me!"

"Where are you?" Caroline spoke, searching the shadows.

"I'm here, help me!" the voice pleaded.

Burble had warned her to trust no one, but this was different; this had to be Ali. Those creatures must have left her here in this forsaken place!

"Ali, is that you?" she called, peering into the shadows.

"You will join her soon enough!" a harsh voice threatened.

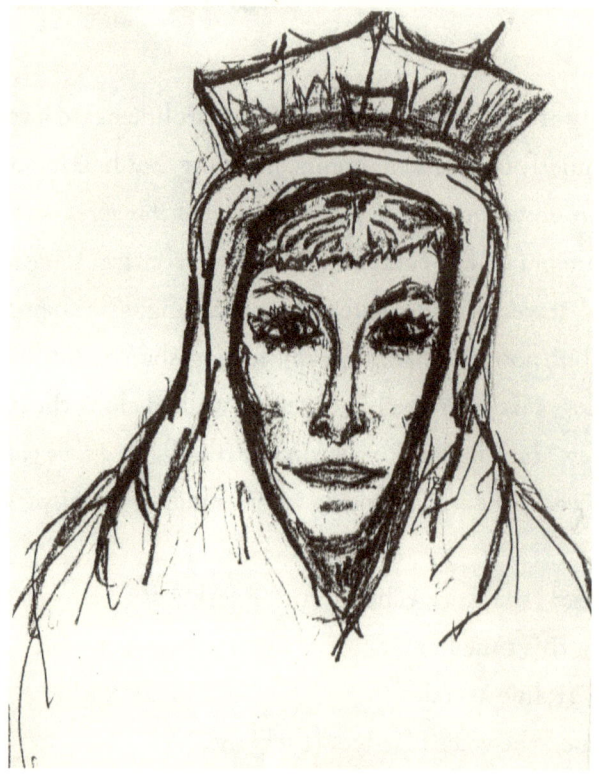

Caroline felt the hair on her neck stand on end as she turned. "Don't be afraid, my dear," a suddenly syrupy voice reassured her.

"Your fear can not save you!"

Caroline shivered as a ghostly figure wearing a long, black cloak materialized from the shadows, moving toward her.

"Well, my dear," the women spoke, "you were fast asleep in your bed last I saw you. You should have stayed there!"

Caroline instinctively took a step back at the woman's harsh tone.

"My shed?" Caroline asked. "You were there?" Her mind raced with a thousand thoughts as she tried to make sense of recent events: Ali in the lantern, the creatures holding her, and the one they served.

"You must be Drizelda," Caroline told the woman.

"It's obvious you are no dimwit, my child; I would be fortunate if my helpers were of your intelligence, but alas, one can't have everything," she told her with feigned regret. "Unfortunately, my dear, you happen to be in the wrong place at the wrong time!" she spoke with a harsh tone, staring at the youngster with evil eyes. "You, my dear, as they say, are a bit of a fly in the ointment, a pill in the potion, a stone in my shoe …" She paused. "Well, I think you get my point," she spoke with a sinister smile. "Unfortunately, my dear, my plans for the future do not include you!"

As the cloaked figure moved toward her, Caroline took several steps back, unsure of the strange women's intention.

"Come now, my dear, it appears your destiny calls, there's really nothing you can do but enjoy the ride!" she cackled.

"Ride," Caroline asked, puzzled.

"Watch that last step, dear, it's a doozey," the woman warned with a devious grin.

She stepped back into thin air, and Caroline understood too late. As terror struck, she struggled in vain to hold on, desperate to keep from falling.

But as she slipped from the cliff's edge, in the mystery of that moment—for just an instant cast adrift on a vast, velvet sea—she could but surrender to the futile struggle and feel only the falling, the dropping, faster and faster! She saw her mother's face, her father's, and then Ali's.

*Ali,* she thought with heartfelt regret, *I'm so sorry; I'm so very, very sorry. I so wanted to save you.*

And in the soundless silence, the youngster dropped out of sight, and into the depths.


The Garden Girl Ponders Her Fate


The lantern swung back and forth as her captors lumbered slowly along the path. The constant swaying motion hadn't helped Ali's tummy any, and she felt a range of emotions: fear, anger, and frustration. She was afraid, but knew she couldn't let fear get the better of her; she felt anger, but knew anger alone would get her nowhere; she was frustrated, but had to keep her wits about her. She had to stay alert and wait for the right time.

The lantern swung, and the oil cloth reeked. She pressed her face to a break in the glass and breathed deeply. The fresh air filled her lungs, and she felt a little better for the time being. Her captors had spoken of the queen with dark powers. She was a maniacal monarch who both envied and despised the garden people. Above all, the queen coveted their knowledge of the magic. With the magic, the dark queen was convinced she would be all powerful ... and rule forever! Her plan was to seduce the young one, offering her riches beyond her wildest dreams. In exchange, Alicia would reveal the complete knowledge of the magic.

Ali's eyelids grew heavy as exhaustion overcame her; she could no longer resist the troubled sleep that waited.

## A Second Chance

From out of nowhere, it snagged her, and, as she dangled from the fortuitous branch, Caroline breathed a heartfelt sigh of relief.

Some time had passed since her nearly fatal fall, and now, as she hung like a puppet on a string, she listened to the dry limb that held her groan in protest. Her mind, overtaxed and a overdone by the recent series of events, could but surrender to the relative boredom of the moment before discovering, with unexpected fascination, the sandal dangling from her big toe, dislodged and hanging precariously, with little left to retain it.

And now, oddly enough, with the sandal's uncertain fate becoming more and more a merciful distraction, she found herself transfixed by the uncertainty of thong's tenuous future. In fact, the sandal had been dislodged not so much by failing the fall as it had by the jolting yank that had occurred following that fateful snag. The jolting stop had stretched her suspenders to the limit before, and, after just a brief hesitation when she was for an instant suspended in space, snapped back, causing Caroline to nearly lose the shoe.

Immediately following the snag, Caroline had, bouncing up and down, resembled a spent jumping jack, but mercifully, as the amplitude of the bounce gradually decreased, she had, at long last, found herself, much to her relief hanging quite still. It had been troubling to be bouncing for what seemed like forever—up and down, down and up—in the dark. Oddly Caroline, had felt great relief in greeting the quiet solitude of being relatively still when it came, in spite of the fact that, not unlike her sandal, her own future remained particularly uncertain and precarious.

It therefore followed that, as the possibility of recovering her sandal diminished, she knew the reality that there was little chance of rescuing the shoe. Combining this with a recently obtained awareness, arguably a newly acquired insight, sublime of essence and imbibed rather quickly during her nearly fatal fall, Caroline now believing wholeheartedly—more than ever, I might add—in that oft unannounced and almost always unpredictable fickle finger of fate. With complete freedom of thought and total absence of malice, and after only a brief deliberation quietly flicked the sandal in question with lithe abloom from her big toe, sending it flip-flopping down and down into the void.

It was in this heightened state of awareness, following the flick of her toe and listening to the serene silence—interrupted only once by the distant thud of the sandal's soft landing on the far-below forest floor—that Caroline remained, hanging quietly, swaying gently in the dim light, waiting and wondering, being very still, and, to the best of her knowledge, as she had so adeptly determined by the sandal's drop, high above the forest floor.

## A Light in the Forest

For a time they had danced on the gentle breeze like fireflies on a warm, summer night, vanishing into the shadows at the least hint of danger.

And so it was, as a hooded figure, stooped and of dark purpose, moved with stealth along the ancient trail, the forest dwellers slipped quietly and quickly out of sight. There was danger in the wood; evil had come, and the black riders were of their mischief. There could be no doubt: it would be in their best interest, as they all agreed, to leave the forest—to disappear. Dark forces were gathering, like a black cloud on the distant horizon.

It was with this purpose in mind, as they gathered to go, that the tremors and rumblings so strong that only legend could compare, began. And now, as the intensity of the rumblings increased the entire land shaking in a blur, there could be no mistake among them: the Great One, as was most certainly apparent, had returned. There could be no other possible explanation.

There had been myths and legends galore, but none of the recent telling of great hoofed creatures of yore—save the hooves of the centaur or Pan himself, as legend would have it—could possibly cause such a ruckus.

Now, as the Great One approached, the creature's thundering hooves shook the ground as he galloped with purpose along the ancient path. And so the forest dwellers waited, wondering. Their fear, for the time being, was diminished by the greater strength of their growing curiosity.

Another Light in the Forest

Uni had entered the forest with stealth, at first but the Great One had warned of imminent danger and he had picked up the pace, accelerating to full gallop, his great muscled body reflecting the stippled light like some careening carousel. He had been running with great speed for some time when he suddenly felt a strong sense that Caroline was close by, stranded, and, more likely than not, in grave danger.

As he slowed from a gallop to a trot to a walk, finally coming to a standstill, Uni peered into the dark and murky wood, listening, searching, and taking several steps. He stopped breathing quietly, listened, and moved on, repeating this maneuver several times until he heard something behind him; but when he turned, he found only shadows.

"Hello?" Uni spoke with an inquiring voice. "Is someone there?"

But again there was only silence.

"Show yourself," he demanded.

But again, there was just silence.

As he moved further into the forest, behind him came another flurry, and with it this time, a flash of shimmering white light. "Caroline, are you there?" he asked. "Caroline, it's me." By now the wood had become completely black, as an ominous dark cloud settled over the forest.

Uni had been feeling his way slowly, when the forest around him exploded again in shimmering white light. With these unexpected illuminations, Uni froze—just in the nick of time I might add—astonished to find himself teetering precariously at the edge of a very high cliff, staring into the depths of a dark abyss.

Recovering from the unexpected surprise of teetering at death's door, he gently and ever-so-carefully stabilized his rather tentative posture. He studied the dark abyss below him. "That next step would have been a doozey!" he said in a loud voice.

He had been thankful for— not to mention fascinated by—the mysterious light that had saved him. Now, as its brilliance dimmed, he began to distinguish, one after the other, many pairs of curious, sparkling amber eyes staring at him from the darkness, waiting and wondering; for, as legend for told, and as the forest dwellers knew, the Great Horn One himself was in fact known to be the keeper of the light.

"That was close, my friends," Uni spoke, turning around slowly in order to make eye contact with as many of his benefactors as possible. "Long live the enlightened ones of the forest," he spoke, for he was of the becoming—and coming to know the ways of the magic. "I will be forever in your debt and forever grateful!"

In the next moment, after hesitating, looking, tilting his head, and listening, Uni leapt from the cliff's edge, into the depths.

Saved?

Caroline had been hanging from the creaking limb, far beyond luck running out, calling, shouting, and screaming for so long that her voice was nearly gone. Now, as she listened in ironic repose to the pure and eerie silence, it finally dawned on her that, magic or no magic, her luck may have, in fact, very well indeed, once and for all, finally run out.

It was in this dreary, rather disheartened state, with her hopes fading and no where to turn—in a manner of speaking—that she was startled by a voice calling to her. "Hey there!" the voice hollered.

Caroline froze, struck with a horrible image of Drizelda coming to finish the job.

"Is that you, Drizelda?" Caroline asked with a shaky voice, gathering her courage. "I know who you are! Your thugs told me your name!"

"Caroline, it's me. I'm here to rescue you!" the voice assured her.

"Uni?" she asked with a sigh. "From the sounds it's making, this old tree is going to break any minute!" she told him.

"It is! It's me!" Uni assured her.

"I'm sure glad to hear your voice, Uni," Caroline told him. "As you can see, I'm in a real fix. I've been saved once by a miracle, but I'm afraid it's going to take another bit of luck to get me out of this tree."

"I have a plan to save you, Caroline," he told her.

"I'm really glad you're here, you know that? But I'm afraid there's not much you can do, my little friend," she replied with another sigh. "How does it look? Do you think I can I swing to the ledge?" she asked. "If I can get up onto the limb I could ..."

"Maybe," he told her as he stepped to the edge, getting closer to his stranded friend. "But that's not part of my plan."

At that very moment, he slipped his long and unique horn under Caroline's suspenders and lifted, ever so carefully, until he could feel her full weight. Satisfied that she was secure, he then backed up slowly, ever so slowly, until she was safe above the ledge. Because of the dim light and the complete skill with which he accomplished the maneuver, Caroline went right on talking as if she were still hanging from the limb.

"Perhaps I should just shake myself loose and hope that I'll land on a nice soft bush!" she suggested.

"That really wasn't part of my plan," Uni said as he lowered Caroline gently onto the ledge. It was the solid ground that tipped her off.

"What, how did I get here?" Caroline wondered out loud as she touched down. "I can't believe it," she spoke. "Now that was magic!"

"That was my plan!" the voice said from directly behind her. As she turned, Caroline's eyes opened wide in disbelief.

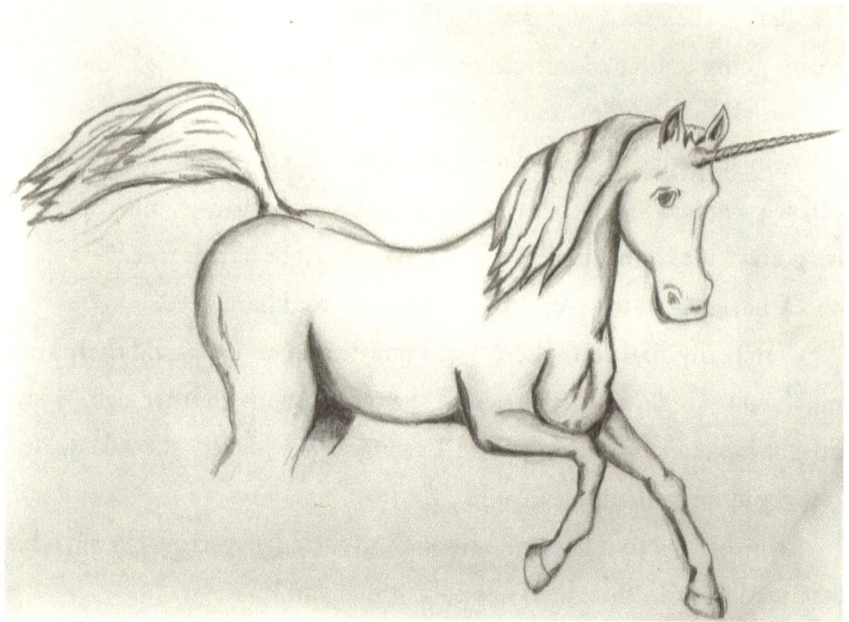

"Who are you, and what have you done with Uni?" she asked in a frightened voice. "Where is he?"

"It is me, Caroline," the great creature insisted. "It really is! It's me!"

"But how?" Caroline gasped.

"I can explain everything," he assured her. "I'm sure glad you're all right! What a relief; I was really worried! I had a bad feeling, and His Largeness told me you were in grave danger and ..." In that instant Caroline, who by now had been rendered speechless, threw her arms around her old friend's now very large and very long white neck, giving him a big hug.

## CHAPTER 8

# Obstacles on the Path

The two companions stood quietly for a moment, feeling very thankful that they were both okay.

Uni spoke, "I hate to rain on our parade, but I'm not sure how we're going to get off this ledge!"

"What?" Caroline asked with a sinking feeling.

"When I heard you calling, I found a trail down the cliff's face, but it ended. Then I saw a ledge below the trail, so I jumped down to it—and then another and so on … I don't think we can go back up the way I came down." He told her, "I'm sorry, that wasn't part of my plan!"

"You mean we're stuck here?" Caroline asked, crestfallen.

"I'm afraid so; at least, for the time being."

At that very moment, they were startled by a rumbling coming from deep within the mountain, and they leaned into the cliff.

"What was that?" Caroline asked as the tremor subsided.

"A quake," Uni warned. "Hold on tight!" he shouted as the rumbling began again. This time it seemed as if the whole mountain was shaking when, without warning, the ledge they were on collapsed, tossing them into a river of gushing mud rushing rapidly down the mountain's steep slope.

"Wooeee! We're in for a ride!" Uni hollered.

"Oh my!" Caroline screamed as they plummeted down the muddied slope. As quickly as it happened, the slide was over, and the two sat, caked in mud. Caroline coughed and spit out mud while Uni shook himself, chuckling and feeling extremely lucky that they had made it down in one piece and were okay.

"That's one way to get off the mountain!" he shouted. "Wooeee, what a ride! That was definitely not part of my plan!"

## The Shadows of Doubt

After a brief rest, the two pilgrims began again, slowly making their way deeper into the dense forest. The thickness of the trees had made going difficult, and they had traveled only a short distance before Caroline stopped again, looking around. "I would sure like to find that sandal," she told him. "It would make it a lot easier going." With frustration in her voice, she said, "I'm pretty sure we passed that trunk just a few minutes ago! It seems like we're going in circles!" She said to no one in particular. "I can't believe it; I'm beginning to wonder if we'll ever make it out of these woods."

"One thing that seems to hold true around here," Uni spoke attempting to buoy his friend's spirits, "is that, sometimes, it just might take the magic in a doubt to help us figure things out!"

"What?" Caroline asked with a sigh.

"Take that thicket over there," he told her "If you look over those trees, it looks to me like there must be a clearing on the other side."

"It sure would be nice to see the sky again," Caroline told him.

"It looks close to impossible that we can make it through that way," he pointed out. "Not only are the trees really jammed together, they're totally covered with vines and bushes. I think I would have just about the biggest doubt of all—with the exception of doubting whether or not we would ever get off that ledge—that we can make it through that mess!"

"You doubted if we could get off the ledge?" Caroline asked him with a raised eyebrow.

"That's it!" Uni exclaimed. "It's got to be. When you've got the biggest doubt is when you've got to keep the faith and rely on the magic to help figure things out!"

"I agree, Uni," Caroline confessed. "I've got a serious doubt whether or not we can make it that way."

"That's exactly why we've got to try!" Uni encouraged. "Keep the faith, girl!" Uni told her with a wry grin. "Hey, farm girl, look over there," he said, pointing to a fallen tree. There, lying under a large log, barely showing, and much to Caroline's relief, was her missing sandal.

## Never Give Up

After retrieving her sandal and taking a short rest, they began again in earnest to tear vines, pushing and shoving their way into the dense thicket. They were struggling for some time before Caroline was so exhausted she had to stop again for a rest.

"I don't mean to rain on your parade, Uni," she told him, "but have you noticed? We're going nowhere fast!"

"You can't give up now, Caroline!" Uni pleaded "We can't give up. I know we've got to make it out of these woods soon. I can 'fale' it!"

## The Master of Shadows

About the time Caroline was ready to call it quits and turn around, the thick undergrowth ended abruptly, and, like magic, the two travelers stumbled into a small clearing, with its thick overhead canopy allowing just a dim light into the small space.

Caroline stood, feeling a bit relieved for the moment, breathing hard and recovering. Her eye was then drawn to a large, dark shape on the far side of the chamber. Suddenly, to her chagrin, she realized it was moving … moving ever so slowly toward them.

"Uni," Caroline whispered, both frightened and intrigued at the same time. . "Over there, do you see it?"

Uni braced himself against his newfound courage.

"Come no closer!" he warned.

"Fear not," said the deep voice.

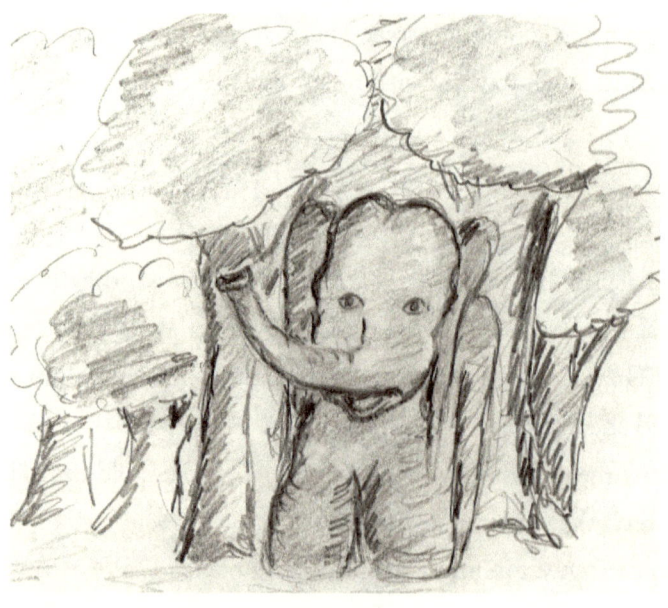

"Who are you?" Caroline asked.

"I am who I am," The voice replied. "I live in the shadows, but am not of them."

"Are you a friend?"

"A friend has many faces."

"I can't see yours," Caroline told him

"To everything, there is a season, young one."

"I've heard that before," Uni chimed in.

"I still don't understand who you are!" Caroline stammered. "Can you help us find the way out of these woods?"

"You could say I'm a bit shady!" the voice said with a chuckle. "Some call me the Master of Shadows. Others call me the Shadow Master! It is the shadows that have brought you this far."

"What about the magic?" Caroline asked.

"The shadows are of the magic," he explained, "but the magic is not of the shadows. Without the light there can be no shadows," he told them.

"So the magic guides us?" Uni asked.

"At times, with shadows," he replied. "Now, you must let go of your fear and doubt and find the path!"

"I'm afraid of what they've done with our friend!" Caroline told him.

"Your friend's destiny lies with your strength," he counseled. "Your fear is of little use; let it go! Now, it is time to find the path!" he said again, with a hint of impatience in his voice.

"We have to rescue Ali!" Caroline spoke.

"At tribal," said the shadowy figure. "Who knows, perhaps it is she who will rescue you; you must travel far on a path less taken," he spoke. "Beware: the path to nowhere may look very much like the path to somewhere. At times, the path may lay hidden as if there is no path at all."

For Those with Eyes to See

"Look for the path not taken!" the Shadow Master advised.

"How can it be a path if it is not taken?" Uni piped up.

"The path to travel lies before you; it is there for those with eyes to see," the Shadow Master counseled as he disappeared into the forest.

"For those with eyes to see," Caroline surmised. "With eyes to see," she said again. "It's hard to believe that we have the eyes to see anything," she told her friend discouraged.

## At Times We Must Doubt What We Believe

"You can't lose heart now!" Uni told her. "You have to doubt your doubt!" he encouraged. "Remember what Ali told us:" he spoke: "'When ya wud be hav'n the biggest doubt, have faith in the magic.'"

"But what if doubting my doubt is in doubt?" she asked.

"Caroline, this is the Forest of Shadows of doubt," he said. "I know it sounds crazy, but sometimes you just have to doubt what you believe and have faith in the magic."

"For those with eyes to see," Caroline repeated, glancing around the clearing. Suddenly, to their amazement, the black shadows were washed away by the noonday sun penetrating the thick, overhead canopy.

"There!" Uni exclaimed, spying a definite opening in the trees. "And over there!"

"And over there!" Caroline joined in. Suddenly, there was a possibility of three paths from which to choose.

"How will we know?" Uni puzzled. "There has to be a way," he mused as he moved toward the opening closest to them. The first path ran straight for a distance and up a hill, disappearing behind a large tree. The second path seemed to go nowhere, but Caroline could see blue sky in the distance. The third entrance appeared to be a dead end. Uni paced, searching for a clue.

"For those with eyes to see, with eyes to see," he mumbled.

"Uni!" Caroline shouted. "Look down this path!" she told him, pointing to the second entrance. Uni peered down the long path squinting against the bright blue sky."

"What do you see?" she asked.

"Is that a cloud?"

"That's what I thought at first!" Caroline replied, obviously excited. "Look again!"

"Oh, I get it now; it's a snow-covered mountain."

"Exactly," Caroline agreed.

"It's nice, Caroline; it makes me think of ice cream, but how does that help us?"

"Perhaps it won't," she answered. "I might be crazy, but the Shadow Master told us to use our head and stop doubting ourselves. Let's look at it this way: the Shadow Master told us, 'A path not taken is there for those with eyes to see.' I know it sounds crazy, but what if he was telling us to take the path with ice traveling to the sea? That would be the ice from the glacier moving down the mountain to the sea. It travels on a path not taken, except by the ice floating in the river down to the ocean—to the sea. Uni, we've got to head toward the mountain."

And so, with their spirits buoyed, Caroline and Uni made their way onto the high plain finally, and much to their delight, for the time being at least, leaving the dark and dingy Forest of Shadows behind them.

## CHAPTER 9

# Light on the Path

Later, the two travelers shuffled along the high plain, each wondering if they would, in fact, ever find Ali. Who were the creatures that stole her in the night? And what of the so-called queen? Imelda? Brunelda? Drizelda? What did she want with their friend? It was all very weird, that was one thing they did not doubt. The trail dipped down for a stretch, and Caroline lost sight of the glacier.

"Uni, I lost track of the mountain." Caroline said.

"Don't worry, farm girl" he told her. "I see it."

"You do?" she asked

"Straight ahead; you'll see it with the next raise of the path."

"Oh, I keep forgetting how much taller you are."

"That's for sure!" he agreed. "It's a lot farther from here to my hooves than it used to be!" he quipped "I like it, though; it's a whole knew perspective. A view from the top! A walk in the clouds! an elevated awareness!" he teased.

"Oh, brother," Caroline said, rolling her eyes.

"Just kidding," he replied. "Just a little humor."

"That's for sure," Caroline agreed. "Very little!"

"Hey!" Uni groaned, pretending his feelings were hurt.

"I'm just giving you some of your own medicine!" Caroline kidded. "Don't you think you need some, 'Your Greatness'? Remember. sometime it takes a little magic to figure it out," Caroline chuckled.

"Wait a minute," Uni groaned. "Sometimes it's not so easy being me."

"What do you mean, Uni?" Caroline asked, concerned.

"I mean I'm glad I'm me. I like being your best friend and all, but every now and then, I wonder. Do you remember the little song your dad used to sing to you?" he asked.

"That was along time ago," she replied. "He stopped singing after my mother died."

"There was the part in the song about being forlorn."

Caroline said, searching her memory, "I can see him holding you up—you were little—and pretending that it was you singing."

"That's it!" Uni said with a grin. "It went something like, 'I was so forlorn ... Until you came my way ... And gave me these three words to say ... 'I love you' ... I do ... Times two ... It's true!'"

"Its funny," Caroline replied, "I can't remember my father telling me that he loved me!"

"That's my point: being able to tell someone that you care about them isn't always easy! One-horns aren't supposed to get forlorn," he pointed out. "His Greatness told me that one horns are keepers of the light."

"I guess I kind of knew that," Caroline told him.

"As we've been searching for Ali, I've been under standing more and more what it means to be a one horn," Uni shared. "It's just seems to be happening, whether I like it or not."

"It seems like you've been changing ever since you stumbled into the meadow that night," Caroline agreed. "It's a big responsibility being the keeper of the light!" she said, lending encouragement.

"His Greatness says it comes naturally to a one horn; that's just it," he confessed. "I'm not so sure I'm suited to be the keeper of anything," he admitted. "After your mother died; I think your father lost his light, at least for a while."

"What do you think the light is?" Caroline asked.

"Ali called it 'the magic.' I guess because when you think about it, being alive really is magic."

"It *is* magic!" Caroline agreed. "Look at you, Uni: you're alive! It's magic! That's all there is to it! Ali always told us to remember the magic!" Caroline told her friend. "I know my father was very sad after my mother died!"

"He really was forlorn," Uni added.

"Wow, look at that, Uni!" Caroline exclaimed.

Ahead, just above the distant mountain, dusting the snow-covered peak with its vibrant colors, was a brilliant rainbow, more vivid than either had ever seen before.

## CHAPTER 10

# A Shining Light

They had been walking on the high plateau for a long while when the path meandered close to the rim of the high cliffs. As they looked beyond the cliff's edge, they saw a vast expanse, and below, an emerald valley that appeared to go on forever. At its depth wandered lazy river.

"It's beautiful!" Caroline shared with her friend.

"I wonder if the trail will lead us down into the valley," Uni said

As they scanned the view, Caroline's eyes were drawn to a flickering light, faint at first, before suddenly shimmering bright in the brilliant sunlight!

"The city of gold, the stories told, is from the stuff of dreams! The riches there, vanish in air, and are never what they seem. The golden star that finds it will guide you on your way, to find the mystery and the magic of the com'n brand new day."

Caroline remembered the story Ali had told her. The shepherd boy had been lured to the village in the valley on the promise that it was made of gold. But he would one day discover that it was just the sun's reflection on the cottage windows and hay-thatched roofs that made the village appear as if it were made of the precious metal.

Much to his dismay, the youth would soon discover that the "village of gold" was in fact very much like his own village. The people there were very much like the people he had left behind. The young man had been very tired after his long journey and, at first, disappointed to discover the truth; but little by little, as he recovered from his journey, he gradually understood what his grandpa had been trying to tell him: It is not the glitter of gold that makes us happy, but rather the glitter of the human spirit true happiness lies within. True happiness is of the heart.

## The Path Not Taken

As they approached the glacier, Caroline could hear the sound of the rushing water. She and Uni watched as the shimmering ice high on the mountain's glacier melted in the warm summer sun, sending glistening rivulets that merged and then merged again in no time at all, creating a rapidly running downhill stream. In turn, as it joined another stream like it, it became, in a remarkably short distance, a rather raging torrent rushing down the mountain's steep slope!

The two had trekked for several hours since seeing the village, and now, with the trail appearing to have ended, Caroline had to shout so Uni could hear her over the sound of the rushing water. "Let's get a drink of at the river, and then we can rest a while." Caroline suggested. "We'll have to hike up the glacier a way to get to the other side of the river. The path must continue there; it seems odd that it would end here!" she told Uni. "What did the Shadow Master tell us?" she asked him. "The path less taken, not taken." As Caroline stepped to the river's edge, the sound was deafening. She looked back and saw that Uni was frantic; he appeared almost desperate, like he was trying to tell her something over the sound of the raging torrent. As she broke through the ice, she realized, too late, that he was trying to warn her!

The water was freezing as she slipped beneath the surface, and she fought hard to get her head above the churning torrent, gasping for air as she sped rapidly toward the cliff's edge.

Without hesitation, Uni ran and flung himself into the fray. He didn't know how, as he felt himself moving faster and faster in the turbulent water, but he knew he had to help his friend. He remembered how odd it seemed that the water racing down the mountain's slope had disappeared before it reached the cliffs edge. Suddenly he understood: he felt himself dropping, whirling round and round while the raging water dropped him into a giant funnel carved by the very torrent that was now plunging down its slippery slopes! Around and around he went, as if riding some crazy merry-go-round. And then, when he least expected it, came the calm, slow motion; he felt himself being flushed into the river. He gasped for air as his head broke the surface.

"Caroline!" he shouted as he spotted her not far, floating face down in the murky water. Glancing quickly at the shoreline and guessing its distance, he took a deep breath and dove beneath the waves, swimming as hard as he could toward her. It seemed like an eternity before he finally felt Caroline's full weight on his back and felt satisfied that she was secure enough. He took a deep breath and swam hard for shore.

He had just scrambled up the rivers steep bank, Caroline clinging to his mane, when he heard a voice next to them. "My God, that's what I'm talk'n about!" the man exclaimed.

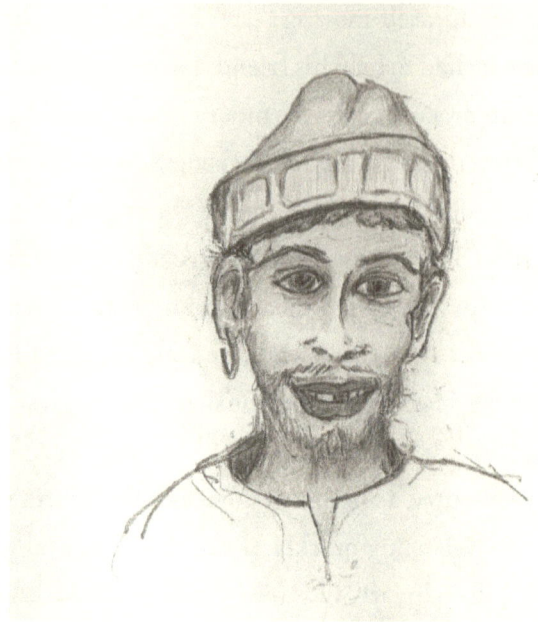

He was a tall black man with bright eyes and a missing-tooth smile. The man moved quickly toward Uni, lifting Caroline from his back and placing the youngster gently on the grass.

"My God, that's what I'm talk'n about!" the man said. "How could you be in the river this close to the falls?" he asked himself. "Unless … unless you came down the funnel?" he said out loud, scratching his head.

"My God, that's what I'm talk'n about! You did; you rode the funnel!"

Caroline coughed and sputtered as she came to … "Uni?" she gasped.

"It's alright young lady," the man told her in a reassuring voice. "Your friend is here, he's right here and we're going to take you to the village." He told her as he hoisted Caroline onto Uni's back and set out with the two of them in tow.

"That's what I'm talk'n about!" the man repeated, simply astounded. "I can't believe it; you made it down the funnel alive!"

## Home Is Where You Find It

The cottage, with its white-washed walls and diamond-paned windows set above bright blue sills, was caped like a grinning garden scarecrow with a thick, hay-thatched roof. Tulips and daffodils bloomed all around its yard.

"The Dancing Dog Inn" was carved in old English on the thick, wood slab that hung above the heavy planked door, and the large black man knocked loudly, pushing against it with his shoulder just as the innkeeper gave a yank.

"My God!" the man said. "I found this young lady in the river beneath the falls! That's what I'm talk'n about!

"Sacre bleu!" The innkeeper exclaimed. "Mimi!" he called over his shoulder. "Please join us!

"Oui oui, Francois; what eez it?" a woman replied. In the next instant, they were joined by a plump, rosy-cheeked woman with twinkling eyes.

"Oh my word!" she exclaimed as she spied Caroline. "Carry ze young lady into ze next room, Claude, and lay her on ze sofa."

"You must rest, dear!" the woman told Caroline. "And take her pony to ze stable!"

## A Disguise for Caroline

Caroline was feeling better when she opened her eyes to see a woman fussing with a garment she had taken from an old trunk.

"How are you feeling, my dear?" the woman asked. "Theze britches will fit you just fine, and theze blouse as well. When you are comfortable in your new clothes, we will roll up your beautiful golden hair; place it on ze top of your head with theze leather cap, and, voila, you will look so very, ah, shall we say, so very ordinary—so, ah, everyday. I was thinking," the women informed Caroline, "that you can be our new helper here at ze inn. You can help in ze stable."

"I truly appreciate all that you have done for me!" Caroline told her, "but I'm on my way to save my friend."

"Yes, of course, dear, but you must regain your strength. Please eat your soup," the woman insisted. "In theze times, the village is no place for a young girl—a child—alone," she told her. "It is important to blend in. As a stable boy, you will go unnoticed; otherwise the wrong people will see a young girl with golden hair and want to know her business. The queen's guard is everywhere, and they have spies. You cannot be too careful! By the way my dear, I am Madam Pompadue. You may call me Mimi," she informed Caroline.

"Hello Madam Mimi," she replied. "I'm Caroline, thank you for helping," she spoke. "As I said; I'm on my way to save my friend."

"The wicked dweazels are no doubt involved!" Mimi guessed.

"The dweazels?" Caroline asked.

"They are the queen's scum!" Mimi snapped. "They are one reason you must wear your disguise, my dear. You cannot be too careful; Drizelda has spies everywhere!"


Queen Drizelda and the Dark Side

"Drizelda?" Caroline asked. "The queen?"

"Yes, my child," Mimi replied.

"She is one who knows no happiness. She is *les miserable*, my child.

She believes that powair, gi-reed, and deceptiown are the *piece de resistance!*"

"I don't understand," Caroline told the woman.

"The queen is a tortured soul," Mimi explained. "It is very sad to realize this woman, this *cherchez la femme* has so completely lost her way. She has been seduced by ze dark side," Mimi continued, "In the beginning, she loved theze land and eets people, but then strange things happened." She went on, "The heir to the throne, Prince Philippe, disappeared under mysterious circumstance without a trace; and it wasn't long after, devastated by the loss of his son that ze king himself, good King Philippe, grew deathly ill. Within the year, both the king and the prince, had vanished from this earth leaving Drizelda, the boy's stepmother and ze remaining heir to ze throne, to declare herself Queen Grand Monarch of all ze land. Slowly but surely, ze kingdom fell under her dark spell! Theeze once wonderful land was now ruled by ze wicked Drizelda and her dweazel henchmen. Ze most hated and feared is ze head dweazel, Obsequious Mooch, known as 'Dweazel the weasel,' who sometimes goes by 'Sigi.' He will stop at nothing to gain Drizelda's favor!"

"How do you know so much about the royals?" Caroline asked.

"We have our ways, my dear!" Mimi told her. "The people of theze land will rise again one day to restore this land to ze peace and ze happiness it once knew," she promised; "the mageek the people once knew with good King Philippe!

"There is a song sung by the bards of the village," she explained. "It is the story of a forlorn soul longing for the mageek," she told Caroline. "At ze risk of offending you, my dear, ze song goes like theze:" Mimi spoke as she began tapping on the table. "It eez called a tap song" she explained.

"Once I had a rainbow I wrapped round ze sun!

"A pocket full of miracles I gave away for fun!

"Now I'm just here sitt'n … waiting for ze tune!

73

"Ze melody of mageek to chase away ze gloom."

A loud knock broke the spell of the moment. *"Pardon, mon ami,"* said a melodic voice. "It is I, my sweet Francois."

"Hallo, hallo, young lady!" the innkeeper said with a broad smile as he entered the room. He was a slight man, short and thin, and his long hair, streaked with gray, was tied up in a ponytail. His nose, oversized and pointed, was straddled by wire glasses, and above his thin upper lip was a bushy, salt-and-pepper mustache.

"This eez Messier Francois Bull-yeah," Mimi told Caroline, as she swung her large arm in the direction of the innkeeper.

"At your service, mademoiselle," the man replied with a bow. "It eez an honor. If there eez anything you need, you must let us know?"

"I was just having the speak's with Caroline," Mimi informed the innkeeper.

"It eez true!" the innkeeper told Caroline, "you cannot be too careful; Drizelda has spies everywhere, and ze dark riders terrorize the people of this land."

"Yes," Mimi agreed. "It eez indeed a sad time. Caroline will dress as ze stable boy, Francois. She will be safe sweeping the stable."

"Meanwhile I will be making plans to rescue my friend!" Caroline informed them.

"Shh!" Francois warned. "You must not speak of your intention without knowing who eez listening!"

"Unfortunately, Francois is right, my dear!" Mimi agreed. "You cannot be too careful!"

"I would like to visit my friend and make sure he is all right," Caroline told the innkeeper.

"Yes, of course, my dear. Put on your boots, and Claude will show you to ze stable."

## To Catch a Thief

Uni felt okay about Jean Claude and the innkeeper. He was thinking about Ali and wondering what might come next and whether or not they would find her when he heard a knock on the stable door.

"Uni, are you there?" Caroline whispered. "I know you're in there somewhere."

"Get away from that stable," a gruff voice shouted from behind her.

Caroline was surprised as she turned to see that the voice belonged to a rather handsome young man, dressed in the same clothes she was wearing. His blue eyes were piercing as he approached.

"Who are you, and what do you want?" he demanded.

"Hello, I'm Carol … ah, I mean … I'm Carl, I'm Carl!" Caroline said again in her deepest voice.

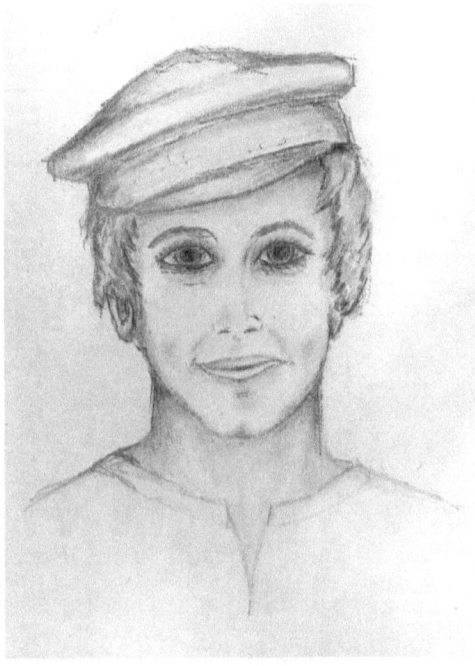

"What are you doing, Carl?" he asked. "There are thieves about."

"I'm no thief, stable boy!" Carl told him. "I'm here looking for my ... ah, ah ..."

"Yes?" the youth asked.

"My friend."

"He looks like a real prize, even with the horn," the youth told her.

Caroline sensed that she was going to have her hands full with this ... this stable boy!

"I told you my name," she parried. "What's yours?"

The boy smiled at the harmless question. "I'm sorry, but there are thieves about My name is Philippe, and I take care of the stables," he told her.

"Well, Philippe," Carl said with a smile, "it looks like I'm gonna be your new helper."

"I guess I could use some help around here," he replied.

## A Proper Introduction

"I see you two have met," Jean Claude said as he entered the stable. "Spud, this is Carl; he is your new helper."

"I'm not sure for how long, *Spud*," Carl told him with a wry grin. "I'm on my way to rescue ... ah ... I mean *find* my friend."

## With Eyes to See

"Philippe," Mimi's voice echoed in the passageway, "it appears that we have guests. The queen's guard is posting a royal decree in the town square and will be taking their lunch at ze Dancing Dog!"

"Okay, Mimi!" Philippe assured her. "I'll be ready!"

"That's quite the animal you have there," Philippe said, giving his full attention to Uni. "I thought they only existed in fairy tales. Aren't they supposed to have magical powers?"

"That's what they say," Carl replied. "I guess it kind of depends what you consider to be magic," she said. "As you can see, he does exist, and to me at least, he does have the magic," she told him in her deepest voice.

"Making this water bucket disappear would show me the magic," Philippe suggested.

Philippe had been telling Carl about the black guard when, to his surprise, he noticed that the water bucket had disappeared.

"What do ya know? The bucket's gone!" Philippe said, laughing. "He made it disappear!"

"It all depends what you consider to be magic," Carl replied. "Uni opened the stable door and picked up the bucket and offered the horse in the next stall a drink of water. He knew you wanted to believe in the magic, so *voila*, he made the bucket disappear … like magic!"

## The Royal Games

A plump man with chubby cheeks and wearing the ill-fitting garb of a royal soldier held the parchment high as he read its contents: "Hear ye, hear ye, good citizens of the realm! Come one! Come all! Let it be known that, on the tenth day of seventh month on the ninth hour of the tenth day, the Royal Games will commence! Let it be known that this great event shall welcome all participants and all upstanding citizens of the realm!"

As the guard lowered the parchment, he turned and spoke to the crowd.

"The featured event, as it is each year, will be the Race of the Royal Steeds! As always, in her great wisdom, the all-knowing Queen Drizelda invites the finest charges of all the land to participate in this great event," he told the crowd. "It is with much ado that I am pleased to inform the good citizens of Drizville there will be a special grand prize," he said, looking down his pudgy nose. "I can assure you ..." At this point the guard hesitated, looking over the crowd. "... that you shall not be disappointed!"

"It iz a clever ploy!" Francois murmured under his breath. "Drizelda fears a faster mount. The Royal Race is ze perfect ploy," he told them. "Every year, horses and riders go missing. Sometimes they show up in ze royal stable, sometimes they just go missing. It is rare that anyone but ze royal guard ever wins ze race."

## The Evil

The queen felt, with a sense of urgency, that the girl was now in her grasp, and she was ecstatic with the possibilities. With the tiny one as an ally, she would rule with complete confidence and power. The secret passage was damp and dripping as she made her way to the dungeon. *She won't last long down here,* she thought as she approached the cold, dark cell.

## The Good

Ali knew that, where there is good, there is evil. *I will live out my destiny, guided by the magic,* she thought. *It will determine the out come of my final journey.* For the first time, she had a strong sense of her own mortality. The heavy dungeon door groaned in protest as it was pushed open, yielding to an echoing thud as it slammed shut. Ali could only listened as the footsteps grew louder.

## CHAPTER 11

# Peasant Boy Bullied

Philippe had bad feelings about the royal guard. He knew they were not to be trusted! They strutted and intimidated, and in the end, they were nothing but bullies!

"Boy!" the guard shouted. "Take my horse and look after him!"

"Yes, sire!" Philippe replied with a hint of sarcasm in his voice.

"Are you mocking me, boy?" the guard growled.

"Never, my liege," Philippe replied, unable to disguise his contempt.

"Watch yourself, boy!" the grizzled guard warned. "Pretty boys like you will find yourself locked away in the queen's dungeon!"

Philippe knew this was no time to take a stand. There would be a better time and place.

### "The Value a Person Gives to Others Depends on his Own Worthiness"

Suddenly, without warning, the guard yanked Philippe from his feet, lifting him into the air and leaving him gasping.

"I told you, boy," the guard swore, "to mind your manners. I wonder just how long a lad the likes a you can hold his breath."

The black bullies were laughing heartily when a sudden hush fell over the crowd.

Uni came from out of nowhere, with his long, rapier-like horn and great muscled body glistening in the noonday sun, and the crowd parted hurriedly as he moved swiftly toward Philippe and the guard holding him.

## Things Are Not Always as They Seem

"Not so fast, rodent!" the guard shouted, but Philippe was having none of it, and he struggled so hard he ripped the shirt from his back while tumbling to freedom.

"Enough!" Lord Mooch shouted over the noise of the crowd. "Let the boy go!" he commanded. "Release him!" He repeated, "Enough! Give the boy his due. He's only a lad!"

The black guard was puzzled. It wasn't like Mooch to interfere with the guard's business.

"So be it!" the guard shouted. "Leave him!"

"Consider yourself lucky, boy; consider yourself lucky!" the guard shouted as the troop galloped off.

The crowd parted further as Uni moved onto the square; he had been estimating the distance between himself and the guard holding Philippe, when to his surprise, the guard released the boy.

## A Royal Crest and a Girl Revealed

"Philippe, are you all right?" Caroline asked in a frightened voice while rushing to his side. It had been a nightmare watching the queen's guard harass the stable boy. It had all happened fast, and then Uni came from out of nowhere, and the head dweazel ordered the guard to release "the boy."

"I'm good," Philippe answered, pulling the shirt back over his shoulders.

In the next instant, without thinking, Caroline threw her arms around Philippe's neck.

"I'm so glad you're okay!" she told him, giving him a crash hug.

Philippe was caught completely by surprise. He couldn't believe it! Carl was a girl? His voice was different and his hair, minus the cap lost in the crash hug, was much longer!

"You're a girl?" Philippe said, at first in a whisper, looking puzzled. "You are ... you're a girl!" he said again, this time out loud, while spinning around and heading toward the stable.

"Philippe, wait!" Caroline begged. "Wait!"

"He will be fine!" Mimi told her over the noise of the crowd; she had come from the Inn when she heard the commotion in the courtyard.

"Uni, you saved the day!" Caroline told him, turning her attention to her friend.

"I'm not sure why they let Philippe go," Uni told her. "I don't think it was because of me."

"Take heem to ze stable, *mon ami*, and feex your hair!" Mimi insisted, handing Caroline her cap. "You can explain yourself to Philippe why you are pozeen as ze stable boy."

## CHAPTER 12

# Destiny's Agenda

The mark on the boy's shoulder had taken Lord Mooch by surprise. How could the boy have survived? The queen would have him boiled in oil if she knew! Fortunately, Drizelda was obsessed with power! She would be with Alicia in the dungeon. The garden girl would give her the secret of the magic … or else!

### Deja Vu All Over Again

Lord Mooch knew the first stable boy from somewhere; the youth was familiar. The large white stallion, the one horn, would make a prize in and of itself. It would be a feather in his cap to present an animal of that stature to the queen. He would be in Her Majesty's good graces for a long while.

But what of the boy and the mark? How could he have returned from the dead? His thoughts raced as he remembered the queen commanding him, all those years ago, to take the youngster, the sole heir to the throne, to the forest to play. He would be lost in the deep wood and never be heard from again.

He had taken the child to the next valley instead and left him in a mountain meadow near a shepherd's flock. He remembered the child sitting among the wild flowers, laughing gleefully as he reached with his tiny hands for the blossoms dancing on the gentle breeze. Lord Mooch had felt remorse for the first time; at least he had left the child alive! The dweazel had hoped that a good shepherd would find the youngster before the wolves did. Drizelda would have him boiled in oil if she ever found him out.

The king was grief-stricken to learn of the boy's demise and blamed himself. Drizelda provided little comfort to her husband, for it was she who was responsible for the devious plot. After months of searching and inquiries and offered rewards, the king, with no hope left, grew ill and died. It was said he died of a broken heart.

Drizelda's ruse had made her queen. It was following these events that the head dweazel, Obsequious Mooch, became the most honorable and obsequious servant of the queen of the realm. It was at the urging of the wicked woman that he raised taxes, encouraged intimidation by the black guard, and squelched all fairs, fun, and festivals. "Working for the queen and the motherland!" was now the motto of, for, and by the people. There was indeed a dark cloud hanging over the valley. The people of Drizland had not seen a rainbow in a very long time!

Lust for Power

The passage had been cold and damp, and the queen was relieved to be in the larger chamber. A single torch cast eerie shadows on the cold, stone walls of the dungeon as a half-starved rat wandered aimlessly across its hard, earthen floor. The lantern was on the far side of the chamber; Drizelda could just make out the soft glow of the fairy princess in the dim light of the dungeon. She remembered her first meeting with the garden girl. She was feisty, full of spirit. *If only my own people could have such moxie,* she thought. She was stubborn, very stubborn, insisting that all things have the magic.

If she could successfully ally with the princess, her power would be unmatched. She would be the most powerful of all. It made her smile—as much as it was possible for the stone-faced tyrant. It hurt to press her lips up at its corners into what the peasants referred to as a grin. Of course, the queen had never heard that a smile is a curved line that often times keeps things straight, but as you will see, it probably wouldn't have helped, even if she had.

They had only recently discovered the garden girl's true identity—what luck, what good fortune! A princess of the fairies! How could they miss? Surely, there could be little doubt, they would have to obtain the secrets of the magic. Drizelda regained her focus as she grew close to the lantern.

## The Pure of Heart Is Not Easily Deceived

It was in the damp darkness that Ali heard a syrupy voice. "Alicia? Are you there, dear? It is your queen. I have come to make sure you are comfortable."

"I am what I am," Ali replied in a quiet voice.

"Yes, my dear, I'm very well aware of who and what you are—well aware," the queen cooed.

"If I wud be so welcome, why'da be keep'n me in this dark and damp place?" Ali asked her.

"Lord Mooch thought by keeping you here, you would be safe," she lied.

As the queen stepped in front of the lantern, she looked to Ali to be in a terrible state. Her face was drawn and pale, with empty eyes perched atop a crooked nose, while her thin lips revealed blackened teeth when she spoke.

"You have what I want!" the queen spat. "The magic!" she hissed, rubbing her boney fingers together.

"You can't be gett'n what you wud be hav'n," Ali explained. "The magic wud be 'n' everthin and everone! Yude be hav'n it as well as I! How can I give ya whut you wud be hav'n?"

"Nonsense!" snapped the queen. And then she thought better of her approach. "You see, my dear," she spoke in a salacious tone, "I understand that you believe the magic is in everyone and everything, and that's fine. What I need you to do is to help me find the magic." With the rather palliative request, Drizelda reached into her robe and withdrew a beautiful gem.

"Isn't it beautiful, my dear? More precious than diamonds or rubies; and this one is so brilliant of luster, so heavenly reflective!"

For a moment, Ali was mesmerized by the jewel and captivated by its beauty. "The stone wud be show'n its glory! That ud be the truth!" she said. "To the glory."

"It is a glorious gem!" The queen agreed. "Consider it yours," she told Ali. "Give me knowledge of the magic, and the stone is yoursssssss." she hissed. "Show me how to rub the stone and bring the magic!" the queen demanded. "I want to know how to rub the stone!"

"The magic wud be 'n' everywun 'n' everythin'!" Ali insisted. "You wude be fale'n it ta be know'n it!"

"Nonsense, my dear," Drizelda countered. "You see, my dear, I know you have the power to release the magic, princess ... princess of the fairies!" she informed her. "It would benefit you a great deal to give me the magic." She explained, "You see, my dear, power is everything. It is power alone that rules! With absolute power there is nothing, I repeat, nothing, absolutely nothing to fear!"

"Everything Is in the Magic!"

Ali was frightened by this woman, who was wild-eyed and crazed with her lust for power, but she had to try to help her understand: power alone was not enough. And how did she know about her secret identity? Only the elders knew the truth. This strange woman did have power.

"The magic wud be 'n' the power, but power wud not be in the magic," Ali began in a simple tone. "Ya can't be know'n it, ya can't be fale'n it, if ya wud be luke'n fer jewels 'n' gems! That ud nary be the way 'o' the magic! Ya must be giv'n upe yur evale ways befure ya can be know'n the magic!" she counseled. "You must give upe!"

"Silence!" raged the queen. "Silence!"

The queen stood, visibly shaken, and stared into the darkness before speaking again, this time in a syrupy tone. "Perhaps some time to think, my dear; surely you must understand, revealing the magic is in your best interest. As you know, my dear, Lord Mooch has been tending to your needs. Unfortunately, he has been called away on royal business," She lied. "However, I'm sure you will lack for nothing," she said with feigned concern, looking at her tiny prisoner with evil eyes.

Drizelda's lips turned up slightly. "We'll see just how long before you beg to give me the magic," she said under her breath. Then, clasping the stone in her fist, she turned and disappeared into the passageway.

# CHAPTER 13

## Farm Girl Meets Stable Boy

"Philippe, you have to understand: Mimi suggested the disguise; she said it would be the best way to stay safe!"

"You're a girl; it's kind of strange, I feel like I lost a friend," he said in a maudlin tone.

"But you haven't, Philippe!" Caroline insisted. "I'm still your friend. Please don't let this ruin things!"

"You're a girl! So long, Carl, nice knowing you!" he said, managing a half-hearted smile. "Philippe," he offered, extending his hand. "It's nice to meet you, Caroline."

"Nice to meet you, Spud," Caroline told him with a smile.

"It seems to me that we have a race to win!" Philippe added. "Are you a rider, Caroline?"

"I rode Uni out of the river into the village after I almost drowned. Does that count?" she asked.

"Oh, sure, that counts ... sort of," he replied. "It seems to me that, with two days to prepare and so much to do, it would make sense to have someone with a little more experience riding."

Caroline couldn't disagree. She knew Philippe had ridden nearly all of his life.

"Spud," Caroline said, a bit hesitant, "I mean Philippe—what is that mark on your shoulder? The dweazel was taken aback when he saw it;

and what about your necklace, the half coin, the symbol of some sort? Where did you get that?" she asked.

## When We Least Expect It, Destiny Calls

"You ask a lot of questions for a girl without any answers," he joked. "Where did you say you came from?"

"I would and will tell you more about me when it's necessary," she said, "but right now, I think knowing more about you is most important. The mark on your shoulder looks very similar to the royal crest of Drizland castle," she continued.

"I wouldn't know," he answered. "I've only seen it in a reflection in the river, and I just thought it was a birthmark, I've always had, it as far as I know."

"What about the pendant?" Caroline asked. "What about that?"

"It was a gift from a long lost uncle. According to my grandfather, it's a good-luck piece and meant to keep me safe from harm."

"Where is your grandfather?" Caroline asked.

"He died."

"Oh, I'm sorry!" Caroline told him.

"He led a good life," Philippe explained. "He was a good shepherd; he raised me well and taught me to fend for myself. My grandfather told me that I was different; that I was meant for greater things, and that in time, that day would come. Since I was very young, he spoke of a city of gold that lay over the high mountain in the far valley. After he died, I thought I might be able to find it so here I am!"

"You are unexpected, Philippe!" Caroline said with sincerity. "I have a feeling that you are more than you know. The dweazel seemed to sense that; it was the mark, the crest."

"So a birthmark looks like a crest?" Philippe scoffed. "It's just a coincidence!"

"And the lucky charm?" Caroline asked.

"It's just that," he replied.

### "To the Victor Goes the Spoils"

"My God, that's what I'm talk'n about!" Jean Claude cried. "You two have some work to do to get ready for the big race! Have you heard what the prize is? That's what I'm talk'n about! A gemstone more precious than diamonds or rubies: a Rainbow Stone!

"We've got to win this race, Philippe!" Caroline told him. "I know it's our best chance to save Alicia!"

"My God, that's what I'm talk'n about!" Jean Claude exclaimed. "Just how do you think you're going to win?" he asked. "You need a very special mount and a very special rider to contend with Drizelda's henchmen. They don't make things easy; they don't play fair. You have to be prepared," he warned.

"They even set ze traps for the unsuspecting challengerrrrs!" Francois spoke as he entered the stable. "Every year there iz many who never finish ze race, while some disappear and are never heard from again!"

"That's not fair!" Caroline protested.

"These are strange times," Jean Claude said in an unusually subdued voice. As Caroline looked at the big man, suddenly he seemed somehow familiar; as if she had known him before sometime … somewhere.

"My God, that's what I'm talk'n about! My God Ah, ah, ah, that's what I'm talk'n about!" Jean Claude shouted, rekindling his enthusiasm as he began describing the race course.

"The race begins at the grand palace in the courtyard!" he explained. "Then it heads across the meadow and leads into the woods. In the woods, it's difficult to catch up or pass on the narrow path. That is why you must gain good position before entering the forest. There are obstacles, tricks and traps, placed by the guard; you must be vigilant at all times!"

"We must help the boy prepare, Jean Claude!" Francois warned. "There iz little time!"

"How did you know Philippe was riding?" Caroline asked.

"It iz easy to see, *mon ami*; ze experience of the stable boy is of value in a race like theeze one. He will ride ze big white?"

"If you're asking if Uni will run in a race like *theeze* one," Caroline teased, "I doubt very much if you could stop him!"

Preparation, Preparation, Preparation

Philippe and Uni rode like the wind! Philippe's strong legs held tight as he clenched a fistful of Uni's bushy mane. Jean Claude had told them to sprint to the edge of the meadow and then slow down, being careful as they entered the wooded trail.

It was shortly after they entered the trees that Philippe found himself flying backward through the air. He was laying motionless for a time on the ground, collecting himself and looking up at the blue sky through the tall trees, when Jean Claude's grinning face filled his view.

"My God, that's what I'm talk'n about!" he laughed. "You fell for the oldest trick in the book. The 'rope-pulled-tight-across-the-trail' trick!" he explained. "Didn't you see it?"

"Not that I remember," Philip answered, rubbing his head.

Mistakes Are Opportunities from Which to Learn

"Welcome to the Royal Race tactics; you must stay low passing through the woods," Jean Claude warned. "The line is just one of many royal tricks. Come on, there's more," he said helping Philippe up.

Jean Claude had many traps set for the duo, and Caroline spent much of her time helping Philippe back to his feet. But finally, Philippe had had enough. "A rest!" he pleaded. "I need a rest!"

"Fantastic!" Francois shouted. "You were magnifeek!"

## "I Really Don't Like Those Guys"

"Good going, Philippe!" Caroline said. "What a workout! Are you okay?"

Philippe sat quietly for a moment, contemplating Caroline's question. "I want—no, I *need* to defeat the black guard, whatever it takes. I won't be bullied anymore." He told them, "Besides, I really don't like those guys." With Philippe's explanation, they laughed together for a few short minutes before getting back in earnest to the preparation at hand.

# CHAPTER 14

## Let the Games Begin

It was early morning when the throaty sound of the queen's flugelhorns proclaimed the beginning of the Royal Games.

"Let the games begin!" shouted the town crier. The morning sun danced on blowing banners while jesters juggled and acrobats somersaulted on the palace lawn. The crowd was already growing in number, anticipating the Race of the Royals.

Philippe, Caroline, Jean Claude, and Uni walked with intent toward the castle. They had risen early, and it would be just minutes now before they reached the palace. Contestants were arriving and making ready. Posted maps of the course were being studied by the contestants.

As Jean Claude had foretold, the race course entered the wood soon after the start. The path then gained rapidly in elevation for several kilometers before emptying onto the great plateau. After a long stretch on the high plain, it ended abruptly, yielding to the giant sand dunes at the plain's edge; great mounds of sand tumbling down to the valley below. These great dunes were, in turn, crisscrossed again and again by the path, the switchbacks, descending down until they reached the valley floor far below. From the bottom of the great dunes, the path then ran along the river's edge, finally, and at long last, reaching the castle.

The forest would be grueling; the trees were dense and the trail narrow, making passage difficult. The high plains would be easier going, but not for long. The great dunes would be treacherous, and it would be difficult to make it down without mishap.

## The Best-Laid Plans

The queen had planned carefully, or so she thought. The Rainbow Stone was the prize, but it would never be given; she had seen to that. If the black guard had done their job, it would be business as usual. The Big Black would triumph once again—against tremendous adversity, of course.

Each year, the traps were set and the obstacles placed; and each year the race run. There were rumors, of course, that the race was fixed and the winner was a "ringer"— a contestant who was allowed to win, but the accusation was never proven.

Each year, the strongest and fastest horses in the realm found their way into the royal stable. If the riders were persuadable, they too could find a place in the queen's legion.

The queen's thoughts turned from the race to her tiny prisoner. She wondered how long the princess could hold out without food or drink.

## Lord Mooch Has a Plan

"Is that the white stallion from the village?" Lord Mooch asked the guard.

"It appears so, my Lord," he replied. "And that is the insolent stable boy standing next to him. The large black man is not to be underestimated!" the guard added.

"I think it will be in our best interest to detain the boy!" Lord Mooch warned.

"How will we do this, my lord?" the guard asked.

"Leave it to me!" said the dweazel. "Leave it to me."

## The Bells

*Ding dang dong! Ding dang dong!*

The bells of the castle steeple sounded the signal: there would be just ten minutes remaining before the great race!

"All riders, mount your steeds and assemble at the queen's starting line. This is the first call to ride!" the chancellor warned. "The great race will begin, following the third call!"

## Everything Happens for a Reason.

"Where is Philippe?" Caroline asked, scanning the crowd.

"He was called to ze registrar," Francois explained. "He was told that all riders must make their mark with ze queen's scribe in order to be qualified to ride in ze race!"

"I don't like the sound of that!" Caroline said in a worried tone. "There are sinister forces at work in Drizland!"

"Perhaps this is a sign, my young friend," Jean Claude told Caroline. "Perhaps you are meant to ride the one horn!"

"There is only one other person I know that calls him a 'one horn.'" Caroline observed, looking at Jean Claude as if she had just seen him for the first time.

"I think you should prepare!" Jean Claude told her, "there is little time, and he is your stallion with the unique horn! And, as you say, he does have the magic!"

"I suppose you're right, Jean Claude," Caroline agreed. "How could Uni run in this race without me?" she asked. "There's just one small problem: I have no experience riding, let alone racing!" she told him, feeling defeated.

"My God, that's what I'm talk'n about! It's been your dream to save Alicia! This is your chance; you've got to take it!" Jean Claude reminded her. "By the way, I happen to know you do have the magic," he encouraged. "You've just got to … got to 'fale' it; that's what I'm talk'n about!" he counseled.

The bells clanged the final warning.

## CHAPTER 15

# Race of the Royals

### The Big Black

The great stallion appeared from out of nowhere; and now, seeing his piercing red eyes and huge, muscled body glistening in the morning sunlight, the crowd parted hurriedly as the Big Black pushed and shoved his way toward the start.

"It eez the Black!" Francois shouted. "He has never been defeated! Against him, you will need the magic! That iz for sure!"

"Remember, *mon ami*," Francois yelled to Caroline in the pre-race melee, "hold on tight, use his mane, and keep your head down after you reach the woods! Trust no one, stay away from the other mounts, and don't get caught between two riders!"

"My God!" Jean Claude exclaimed. "That's what I'm talk'n about! Remember the magic!" he encouraged. "Hold on tight and fly like the wind!"

"I know we can do it, Uni!" Caroline shouted in her friend's ear.

"You can do it, my one horn friend!" Jean Claude encouraged.

Suddenly Uni realized where he had seen Jean Claude before.

### The Race Begins!

"On your mark!" the starter shouted. "Ready …"

And with the swoosh of the royal banner, the race was on!

Uni leapt forward, his powerful legs driving hard and Caroline holding tight. They were moving rapidly ahead of the rest of the pack when two guardsmen suddenly appeared out of nowhere, pushing their mounts against Uni and forcing him to slow. In the commotion, the Big Black sprinted ahead, separating himself from the rest of the pack.

It was then that Uni began to "fale" it! "Hold on, Caroline!" he shouted.

In the next instant, he jammed on the brakes letting the two assailants' momentum carry them forward. As they slowed to intercept him again, he turned on the speed and galloped past them, leaving Caroline with nothing to do but wave good bye.

The damage had been done, however, and now, with the Black running far ahead and approaching the woods, Uni and Caroline pushed hard to catch up, knowing that it would be tough going in the forest.

The Path Narrows!

The Black had disappeared just seconds before they reached the forest, and now, as they galloped onto the wooded trail, there was a swoosh above Caroline's head as Uni pushed them up the slope with his powerful legs. As Jean Claude had warned, it was tough going in the trees. He had been right—the trail was steep and very narrow

Because the path ran straight at times, Uni and Caroline caught glimpses of the Black pushing hard up ahead. Just as it seemed the steep trail would never end, they broke out of the woods to find themselves galloping rather easily on the great plateau.

*Wow, this is beautiful,* Caroline thought as she spied the Black. *You can see forever!*

In the next instant, Caroline felt herself flying through the air, and everything went black. The trip line had caused Uni to stumble badly. He recovered from his nearly fatal fall, fearing for his friend, who lay motionless on the ground.

Caroline had been knocked out, and now, as she began regaining consciousness a gentle voice called to her. "Caroline? Caroline?" it whispered.

She slowly awakened, peering into the black void; Caroline's heart soared as her mother's smiling face floated toward her, and she was further thrilled to see her father—her father!— holding up a little Uni and … singing. As she listened to the tune, it faded in and out, but seemed, somehow, oddly, familiar.

"I'm Unis the Unicorrrrrn," the song began, "And I was so for … lorn; until one day you came my way; and helped me … chase my … cares away; and …"

As she awakened further, it was her mother asking, "Are you okay, sweetheart? Are you okay? Are you all right?"

Then it was Uni asking, "Are you okay, Caroline?"

"Oh," Caroline moaned, opening her eyes. "What hit me?"

"It was a trip line," Uni said with concern. "Are you okay?"

"I think so," Caroline told him, rubbing her head.

"It's a miracle! You're all right!" he told her. "You hit hard."

"Uni!" Caroline cried excitedly. "The fall! I saw you! I know who you are! I remember who you are!"

"What a relief!" he said. "For a minute there; you had me worried."

"I've known you almost my entire life, right?" she asked.

"True," he agreed.

"It's funny what we forget and don't remember," she said with a laugh. "When I hit my head, it came back to me, like jostling an old memory!" she explained. "You remember my mother? She died when I was young. She asked me to keep her close in my heart and in my dreams. When I hit my head, I saw my mother!" Caroline continued, "She was telling me that I would be all right, that she loved me, and that I should listen to my father ... my father, Uni! I saw my father! Not only did I see him, I could hear him; he was holding you up and singing. I can't believe I forgot!" she told him as she began singing in a quiet voice.

As Uni listened, the tune did seem somehow, oddly familiar.

"I'm Unis ..."

"Unis?" Uni interrupted.

"...the unicorn," Caroline sang. "Unicorn Uni!" she told her friend with a chuckle. She continued, "And I was so forlorn; until one day you came my way; and helped me chase my cares away; and gave me these three words to say; I love you, I love you, times two, I do, it's true ... *I love you!*"

"Don't you see Uni?" she asked. "In my father's eyes, you were, ah ... are a unicorn," she explained. "When my mother died, he stopped singing. My father knew my mother was sick, and he stopped singing. That's when my mother told me that you were Uni with the unique horn. She loved you, she loved me, and she couldn't sing my father's song. She knew he would have to find it again on his own. When my mother died, my father stopped singing. You're a unicorn, Uni! It wasn't Uni with the unique horn; it was Unis the Unicorn!" Caroline chuckled, still astonished by the realization. "A unicorn, Uni! You're a genuine unicorn! I don't know why I didn't see it before!"

"For everything, there is a season!" he chuckled. "I have to admit," he told her, "I didn't expect to be enlightened by a girl falling on her head! Okay, so I'm a unicorn ... with a unique horn ... who used to be forlorn, according to the song; what exactly does that do for us?" he asked.

"Don't you see, Uni? It means that you are of the magic and the light," she explained. "I know my father has seen the light, he's just forgotten! I know he'll remember," she continued, "especially if we can win this race and save Ali. You are of the magic, so we have a great chance to win, which means we have a chance to save Ali, which means ..."

"Hold on, farm girl," Uni interrupted. "Speaking of the race and saving Ali, we have to get going right now!" he warned. "The Black is miles ahead, and I don't have a clue how we're going to catch him—or who's going to be catching us for that matter!"

"You don't?" Caroline asked, looking at her newly enlightened friend out of the corner of her eye.

"Don't be telling me that, because, in your eyes, I'm a keeper of the light, and I'm going to zoom past the Black like he's standing still," Uni hollered as Caroline hopped up on his back. "Somehow, I don't see that happening."

"We have to get going, Uni!" Caroline warned, urging him on.

"I'm glad you finally noticed!" he shouted, straining hard to reach a gallop.

In a short time, they were running full speed, in pursuit of the Black. *He's so far ahead,* Caroline thought, *it will take a miracle to catch him.* And so, determined, they galloped on, across the high plateau, closing rapidly on the great dunes.

"Jean Claude said the switchbacks look like they go down the dunes forever!" Uni shouted to Caroline. "I think we can make up some ground there!"

"You see, Uni, you really are a unicorn; your magic is working already," Caroline told him.

"One more thing, Caroline," Uni hollered over his shoulder. "Do you remember when I said, in former times, I couldn't talk, but I could listen?"

"Yes!" Caroline answered.

"I think it's a good time to tell you about Ali; she is special."

"I know!" Caroline assured him.

"She is those things the dweazels said, and more!" he continued "She made the dark queen promise not to harm you if she agreed to go to Drizland. She was sent to help you by the people of Briar Moore; if she succeeded, it was all to be part of her becoming. She was 'to cume ta know the magic'! Instead, she went with Drizelda—to save you!

"Oh, and, Caroline, she's not just Ali the garden girl. She's the Fairy Princess Alicia!" he told her.

They had been moving along the great plateau for a while when the Black abruptly disappeared from view.

"He's reached the switchbacks!" Uni shouted over his shoulder

"Never Give Up!"

"It will take him a while to make it down!" Caroline shouted. "After that, it won't be long until he'll reach the palace!" They galloped on with added determination. Finally, to their relief, they reached the edge of the high plain.

"Amazing," Caroline exclaimed as she looked out over the valley. "It's beautiful! there are the switchbacks, and the Black looks like he must be halfway down!"

"I think we might have a chance to catch him!" Uni told her.

"You're really fast, Uni, but are you *that* fast?" Caroline asked, feeling defeated. "Unless … unless you've got some 'unicorn magic' up your sleeve?" she asked, feeling a bit more optimistic.

"Not really!" he answered. "And I don't have sleeves," he told her. "It's called basic mathematics; the shortest distance between two points is a straight line!"

"Straight line," Caroline repeated, raising her eyebrows. "Are you thinking what I think you're thinking?"

"We can do it!" he encouraged. "Just hold on tight, and I'll take care of the rest!"

"This has got to be the unicorn in you talking," Caroline told him. "I sure hope you know what you're doing, Mr. Unis the unicorn!"

"Let's do it then, on three," he encouraged. "One … two … two and a half … threeeeeeee!" he shouted as he leapt over the edge onto the great dunes. "Oooooh … weeeeeeeeee! Here we gooooooooooo!" he cried as sand exploded all around them.

"It's like flying!" Caroline shouted. In fact unbeknown to her, they actually were flying—for flying is a power a pure and selfless unicorn does subscribe both secret and sacred; forever undisclosed at risk of losing, even to a mistress of dreams.

Uni's hooves were barely touching the tops of the great dunes now as the two kindred spirits flew down the sandy slope, closing rapidly on the Black and his unsuspecting rider.

### Boredom, a High State, Can Lead to Bliss

For the black stallion, it was business as usual—get a big lead, whatever it took; hold it; and win the race. *What a yawn, it's always the same. I wonder what it would be like to run in a real race*, he thought. *I'm sure I could hold my own, I just need a chance!*

Suddenly, there was an explosion of dust and sand ahead, so thick it made it hard to see. With this surprise explosion, the black's rider slowed, not knowing what to think, just as Uni leaped from the swirling cloud with Caroline on his back

"What!" the rider shouted. "We were miles ahead!"

*Fantastic!* the Big Black thought, *A real race after all!*

Uni and Caroline were ecstatic; they had made it all the way down without mishap!

"Amazing, Uni!" Caroline shouted. "That was great!"

But there was little time to celebrate, as they spied the Big Black, with his thundering hooves bearing down on them.

It took all of Uni's energy to get them up and running fast enough to avoid being trampled. In the next instant, the two steeds were running flat-out neck and neck, and the Black was finally having fun. As they approached the palace, word spread: "It's neck and neck! It's anyone's race!"

### The World Is as You See It

With the rumble of anticipation in the crowd, Lord Mooch turned to see what the commotion was all about.

"Neck and neck!" a black guard shouted. "They're just minutes away!"

Lord Mooch told himself not to panic. *What now?* There had never been a challenger before. He had seen to that. His mind raced; what would the queen think? What would she do? He took a deep breath and told himself to stay calm. The crowd grew louder as the black and white appeared on the horizon. Should he declare the Black the winner, regardless?

"They're coming!" the grounds men shouted. As he hurried to the finish line, Lord Mooch knew there was only one thing he could do.

### The Finish

Uni pushed hard, gasping for air, while the Black frothed at the mouth, his eyes bulging. The two steeds were running flat out now, straining hard as they galloped on with reckless abandon.

"Come on, Uni, you can do it!" Caroline shouted. "You can do it!"

The ground trembled, and heads turned as the galloping steeds raced rapidly toward the finish. They were neck and neck, and as they approached the castle, Uni had a feeling it would be too close to call; he knew there was only one thing left to do.

With the swoosh of the flag, the great race was over, and the exhausted contestants slowed, gasping and gulping air as they recovered.

The crowd was going wild; no one had ever defeated the black stallion! The field was awash in speculation. People cheered for no apparent reason.

Lord Mooch was shaken; he had to make the call, and he knew he couldn't win. He would just have to make the best of it.

## To Close to Call

"Ladies and Gentleman," Lord Mooch spoke with authority as he addressed the crowd. "It is with great pleasure that I announce the winner of the Queen's Race," he dramatized. "This was a contest the likes of which has never been seen before!" he continued, stretching the moment to the best of his ability. "Today's race was, without a doubt, a contest extraordinaire! The race of the decade ... no ... I have to say the century—yes, that's it: the century!" he added with theatrical exuberance. "It was unbelievable, beyond compare!"

"Quit stalling!" someone shouted.

"Tell us, who won?" demanded another.

"Yes, who won?"

Mooch knew he could stall no longer.

"Oh, that, yes, ah yes, the winner," he spoke. "Yes of course. The winner is ..." he said, hesitating, his eyes darting back and forth. "By the tip of a horn ..." At this point, the crowd exploded with cheers; making it nearly impossible for anyone to hear. "... is ... 'The Big White!'" he said quickly, glancing nervously over his shoulder.

## CHAPTER 16

# The Grand Prize Awarded

## A Sticky Wicket for Lord Mooch

All her life the queen had improvised, and she would do so now; there was no way anyone would keep the most precious gem, the coveted Rainbow Stone! It was she who would gain the secrets of the stone, and no one else! As she sat in the royal chamber, awaiting the winner of the race, she whispered to Lord Mooch.

"You've really botched it this time, Mooch. You'll pay for this!"

"I can explain, my queen," Mooch replied. "It was the boy."

"The boy?" she asked.

"Yes, the boy!" he whined.

"The boy?" she snapped, obviously irritated.

"Yes, the boy!" He repeated, shaken.

"Will you stop that!" the queen demanded.

"The young prince has returned," he blurted out.

"Where is he?" she asked.

"He's safe," Lord Mooch replied, not really knowing. Obsequious had intended to capture the boy and either incarcerate him or perhaps make a deal with him. He was, after all, Head Minister Obsequious Mooch, and he did have his connections. If he played his cards right, perhaps it would be he who would help the young prince regain the throne,

"I'll deal with you later, Sigi!" the queen hissed.

In the next moment, the tall doors of the grand chamber were opened with all the pomp and circumstance worthy of such a special royal event.

The queen sat stone-faced on the throne, for now she would hide her anger and play the role of the benevolent ruler, knowing, deep in her cold heart that she would never give up the stone.

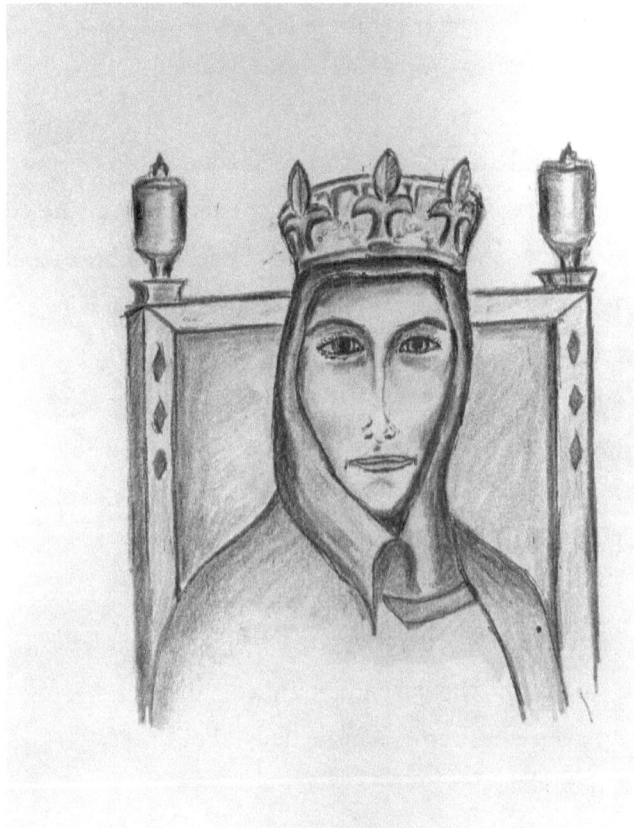

Caroline Reveals her True Nature

The trumpets sounded as the chamber lord prepared to announce the winner and new champion of the Race of the Royal.

"Ladies and gentlemen!" he said addressing the crowd. "I am privileged to present to you the winner of the royal competitions, the victor of the contest beyond compare!

"I give to you!" he spoke with a full voice: Carl of Morning Cloud and his fine mount, the great white ... ah, ah ... one horn!"

"He's a unicorn!" Caroline whispered, "Unis the Unicorn!"

The chamber lord cleared his throat and began again. "Ladies and gentlemen, I give to you the winner of the Race of the Royals: Carl of Morning Cloud and his magnificent steed, Unis of Unicorn!"

"Actually my lord, he is a unicorn," Caroline told the chamber lord, but the noise was already quite deafening as the crowd roared with wild enthusiasm. As Caroline and Uni entered the Grand Hall, slowly making their way down the aisle toward the queen, Caroline couldn't help but smile, it was like a dream! In fact it, *was* a dream! It was hard to believe that they had actually won. The best part of all was that Caroline was actually beginning to "fale" it. She was just that much closer to finding Ali.

## Guided by the Light!

The trumpets sounded, *da da daaaa ... da da daaaa!* The crowd cheered, and confetti filled the air! There was a sense of joy and merriment; an unknown, an underdog, had actually won. How was it possible?

As she approached the queen, Caroline noticed, from the corner of her eye a black guardsman waving frantically, and he appeared to be waving at her. She didn't understand until the guard pulled the bandana from his face.

"Philippe," Caroline mouthed, recognizing the face behind the mask and thinking better than to say it aloud. *Philippe, Philippe! You're all right,* she thought to herself, *What could have happened?*

As the procession continued, Caroline had a realization: she was tired of being a boy, and with one quick move, she removed the hat from her head, letting her golden hair fall past her shoulders. A hush fell over the crowd, the queen gasped, and Francois's chin dropped, while Jean Claude applauded, chuckling to himself.

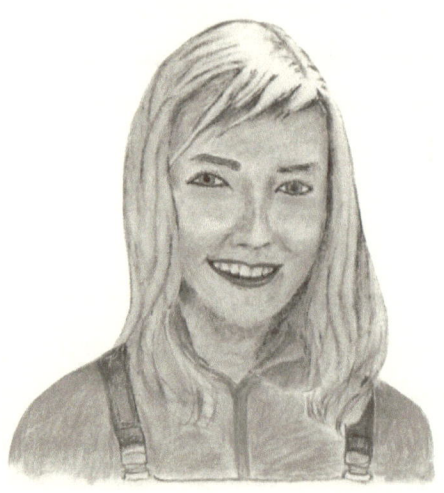

There was a brief pin-drop silence before the crowd began cheering once again with great enthusiasm. In a short time, someone started a chant, "Carl, Carl, Carl!" And then, because it was obvious that Carl was in fact really a girl, someone began a second chant sounding off with a question, "Carl? Carl? Carl?"

### The Calm before the Storm

The queen glared at Lord Mooch. She was sure she had disposed of this insolent girl; she had seen her fall from the cliff with her own eyes!

"See what you've done, you idiot?" she snarled "You'll pay for this!" She sat back and waited, with the ends of her lips rising ever so slightly—her attempt at a benevolent smile! *How can people smile?* she thought. *It's so very uncomfortable.* She had to think; the girl had become powerful.

The crowd continued to chant "Carl? Carl?"; shifting to "Uni, Uni," and then back to "Carl, Carl!" As the precession came to a halt in front of the queen, both Caroline and Uni gave a respectful bow.

The hall fell silent as the queen surveyed the crowd, feeling the mood of the moment.

"Welcome, my dear," the queen said with a patronizing tone. "You and your magnificent steed have done what no one … ah, woman … ah, or should I say no one, period, has ever achieved. You, my … ah …"(The queen was still adjusting to the fact that Carl was a girl. "… ah … my dear …"

"Caroline," she whispered to the queen. "Caroline, Your Majesty."

"You, Caroline," the queen spoke, looking over the audience, "have won the Race of the Royals."

At this point the audience went wild cheering loudly, calling "Caroline! Caroline! Caroline!" Caroline turned, raising both hands to acknowledge the crowd.

As silence once again befell the court the queen continued, "You, Caroline, and your magnificent steed have won the most prestigious race of the realm, and with it, the most precious gem in the land: the most incredible and beautiful Rainbow Stone!" She surveyed the crowd, hiding her true feelings. "According to myth, the stone holds many secrets and is known to bestow wisdom and power upon its owner," the queen told the court. "Power not to be taken lightly," she added. With that, the queen, hiding her reluctance to part with the stone, motioned for Caroline to come forward and receive the treasure!

As Caroline knelt before the queen, the monarch spoke. "Caroline of … ah … ah …" the queen stammered.

"Morning Cloud, Your Majesty," Caroline reminded her. "Morning Cloud."

"Caroline of Morning Cloud," the queen began again, addressing the court with her most regal voice, "you have done well." She placed the lanyard with the stone around the young champion's neck. "You have won the Race of the Royals, and are now the Champion Extraordinaire of this land!

"Behold!" the queen spoke. "I give you Caroline and the magnificent gem, the rare jewel, the ever fabulous, ever glorious, Rainbow Stone!" The crowd went wild, cheering with gay abandon as Caroline stood and turned toward the audience, holding up the stone.

It had been only a few moments after receiving the stone and acknowledging the crowd that the young champion once again raised her hand, this time asking for quiet. As the crowd grew silent, Caroline began, her confident voice resounding through out the chamber. "Your Majesty and people of this land, it is indeed an honor to have been a participant in this great event, and I am overjoyed to have won!" she said with enthusiasm. "You see, it was of the utmost importance that Uni and I win today!" she continued, "for I am on a quest ..." The crowd murmured. "... to find a friend. I have every reason to believe that she is here, being held against her will in Drizland Castle. The stone that hangs from my neck tells me that she is here. My friend is the Fairy Princess Alicia of Briar Moore Garden, and with due respect, I would appeal to Her Majesty to release her."

With that, the crowd cheered with gay abandon then started another chant: "Alicia, Alicia! Alicia!"

## Do Fairies Exist?

Lord Mooch raised his hand, calling for order. As the crowd grew silent, the Queen addressed them.

"Isn't it true that fairies exist only in fairy tales? Have you seen one lately?" she asked. "Myths, legends, and stories are filled with all kinds of make-believe characters, but this is here and now, and I assure you, people of this court, there is no fairy princess in Drizland Castle! The idea is absurd!" the queen said with a huff.

"The princess is here, and I will find her!" Caroline insisted.

"Of course you will, my dear. Of course you will!" the queen answered, placating the young girl and the ever-interested crowd.

"I know she's here, Your Majesty, I wear her stone!"

At this point, the crowd began talking rapidly among themselves. Following a brief pause, Caroline raised her arms once again asking for quiet. "Your Majesty," the youngster pleaded, "please, Your Majesty and the people of this court, there is another more pertinent topic that I must bring to the court's attention—a topic of vital importance to the future of this land and its people!"

"I think you have said quite enough!" the irritated monarch snapped.

"Let her speak!" someone yelled.

"Yes, let her speak!" the crowd encouraged. With the outburst, the black guard stood to attention.

Sensing the mood of the moment, Drizelda saw an opportunity to put this young rebel in her place. After quickly conferring with Lord Mooch, she asked for quiet.

As the crowd hushed again, the queen spoke. "Very well, my dear," the queen said, turning to face the people of the court. "Let the people of Drizland know that your queen, in her wisdom, in her benevolence, and with her utmost compassion, has decided, in fact, insists that this young lady, Caroline of Morning Cloud, has her say!"

## Will the Rightful Heir Please Stand Up?

"Yes, Your Majesty, thank you. I would now like to point out to the court that, in truth, at this moment the rightful heir to the throne of Drizland Castle …" At this point, Caroline hesitated. "… does not …" She hesitated again. "… sit on its throne!"

With that, the crowd drew a collective breath and began speaking rapidly among themselves. Meanwhile, the queen's stone-cold gaze was fixed on the young girl.

"That is ridiculous!" the queen snapped. "Absurd!"

"Let her speak!" Someone in the crowd yelled.

"Yes, let her speak!" cried another.

Soon the entire court was demanding that the girl be allowed to continue. After Lord Mooch approached the throne and conferred briefly with the queen, she turned again to address the audience.

"Very well," said the queen, obviously flustered, staring with angry eyes at the upstart girl. "You may continue."

"Thank you, Your Majesty. I would now submit to this court," Caroline continued, "that the rightful heir to the throne, the son of the true patriarch, good King Philippe, the youngster who disappeared mysteriously all those years ago, is at this very moment, alive and well in this very hall! In addition, I would point out to this court that it is the crest indwelled on the young man's shoulder that will be the absolute proof of his identity!" With Caroline's explanation, the crowd breathed a collective breath and then once again began talking among themselves.

"How could this be?" asked one.

"Is this possible?" said another.

"How shall we know?" asked a third.

## The Truth Cannot Be Denied

It was Lord Mooch who spoke first after the noise subsided. "Hear, hear! It is obvious that this is a clever ploy, a ruse, a deception, an attempt to discredit Her Majesty!" he shouted. "Anyone can claim to be 'the long-lost prince,' and everyone knows the story of him going missing all those years ago!" With that, the head dweazel turned to confer a few moments with the queen before once again addressing the audience.

After speaking with Lord Mooch, Drizelda's countenance changed. Her cold stare had been replaced with the hint of a smile, while her eyes belied an overconfidence. The dweazel once again addressed the court. "If this rightful heir to the throne does exist, of course the queen welcomes him with open arms! All of us remember the tremendous grief the queen suffered when the youngster disappeared under mysterious circumstances all those years ago. How difficult it was for the queen, after such heartbreak, to assume the throne! It was no secret how hard the good queen struggled, after the king's death, to make Drizland what it is today!" Lord Mooch blabbed to the crowd in an exceptionally obsequious tone.

"What a joke!" said one under his breath.

"Yeah, she worked so hard to rip us off!" said another.

Lord Mooch called for quiet and straightened before taking a step toward the audience. "Let it be known that it is the wish—no, the will of the all-knowing and benevolent queen that the son of good King Philippe, the heir to the throne of this kingdom, if, in fact, he does exist, come forward and acknowledge this assembly!"

## Will the Real King Please Stand Up?

There was a brief silence, a hesitation, and then a slight commotion in the audience as a black guardsman stepped from the crowd and walked toward the queen. The crowd murmured as the guard approached the throne, but it was the queen who spoke first.

"You are the son of King Philippe?" she asked

"I am," the youth replied.

"He can't be the rightful heir!" another youth spoke as he stepped from the crowd.

"I am!" said a second.

"That can't be!" cried a third. "I am!"

"Well, well, well, there appears to be more than one rightful heir to the throne!" the queen observed, her voice filled with sarcasm.

## An Imposter Gets the Upper Hand

It was easy for Caroline to see the deception as she edged closer to Philippe. It was obvious that Lord Mooch, knowing Philippe might approach the court, had taken precautions. Caroline quieted the crowd with a raised hand as she spoke. "There is a way to determine the rightful heir!" she insisted.

"Don't be ridiculous, my dear. Your little ploy has been exposed, it's over!" the queen gloated.

But Caroline spoke out with conviction. "There is a mark, an indwelled mark, on the left shoulder of the true prince. It is a well-depicted image of the royal crest!" Caroline insisted. At this point, she turned to Philippe and, looking rather sheepish, pulled his shirt up, revealing the image. The crowd gasped.

"This proves nothing!" Lord Mooch snapped. "Come forward," he ordered, pointing to the second youth. When that youth stood before the queen's assembly, the dweazel pulled that youth's shirt up, exposing a similar mark. It was the same for the third. Now the court was full of questions and there appeared to be no answers.

Caroline once again raised her arms, asking for quiet, but it was Drizelda who spoke first. "Your little ploy has failed, my dear. You should take your prize and go before I lose my patience!" she warned with a threatening gaze.

Caroline swallowed hard, shivering involuntarily as she stared into the Queen's angry eyes. At the same time, she remembered Burble's advice from the night so long ago: "You must let go of your fear, Caroline; use it to your advantage."

As the hall fell silent, Caroline was cast back into the moment, feeling the eyes of the court staring at her, waiting, watching ...

Myths and Legends, Songs of the Universe

Swallowing, hard she began, "As legend would have it, when he was very young, the prince was given a special pendant by his father, the good king. The pendant was meant to protect the prince always," She informed the court. "That pendant, at this very moment, hangs from the neck of the true prince!" she told the court in a confident voice. "The pendant has not been duplicated. There is only one!"

The queen stared at the head dweazel with a questioning, angry gaze.

Lord Mooch scoffed at the girl's statement. "That is absolutely absurd!" Mooch told the people of the court.

"The pendant," Caroline continued, "was given to the prince under the most secret of circumstance. Its existence known to only a few!" she explained, looking at Madam Pompadue.

"Balderdash!" cried Lord Mooch. "You're making up stories as you go!"

"Let her speak!" cried a voice in the crowd.

"Yes, let her speak!" shouted another.

"Yes, let her speak!" It was Queen Drizelda, sensing the futility of Caroline's situation. Queen Drizelda would now play the role of the understanding, benevolent ruler. She would let Caroline continue with this nonsense for a while longer—but not too much longer. The queen knew there could be only one outcome at the end of this day: she, and she alone, would be queen.

### Wisdom, a Gift from a Father

"Thank you, Your Majesty," Caroline spoke with conviction. "As I said, this pendant was so very special. It has, in fact, protected the young prince all these years, as I believe it will protect him now. It has served its purpose and will now give absolute proof to the court that this is, in fact, good Prince Philippe!"

The crowd murmured as the queen's eyes darted from the crowd to Lord Mooch and back to Caroline. Lord Mooch fidgeted, growing more concerned as this nuisance of a girl continued.

"The king, in his wisdom, seems to have anticipated well for future possibilities. Perhaps he understood somehow that it would come to this." Caroline informed the members of the court.

"Come, my dear. Your eloquence is admirable, but can we move along?" the queen pleaded. "I have a kingdom to run!"

"Your Majesty and people of this court, I would now ask that we examine the very throne occupied by the queen herself!"

With Caroline's suggestion, the queen harrumphed in disgust. "What does that have to do with anything?" she demanded.

"Yes, what does that have to do with anything?" Lord Mooch parroted.

"Quiet, Mooch!" the Queen snapped.

## The Prince Who Would Be King

"The throne must now be the focus of the court, Your Majesty," Caroline told the court in a loud voice, "for it is the throne itself that would know the prince who would be king." She explained, "I would now like to bring your attention to the very top of the throne itself. At its height, there is an oval. Inset in the oval is the royal crest of Drizland Castle, cast in gold. At this time, I would ask the people of the court to examine the oval." Reluctantly, the queen stood and turned to look at the crest.

The people moved quietly closer. "It is nearly undetectable unless someone points it out as I am doing now," Caroline explained. "If we examine it more closely, you will see that the golden crest is no longer complete, but, in truth, is precisely, as you will see by looking closer, just half of its former self. The other half of the seal, at this very moment, hangs from the neck of the true prince. I would now ask the true prince of this land to approach the throne and place the missing half of the seal into its rightful place."

There was silence as all eyes went from one imposter to the other. After a brief hesitation, Philippe stepped forward, removing the pendant from his neck. The queen stood still as a statue, her eyes darting from the youth, to Lord Mooch, and to Caroline.

After hesitating for a moment, Philippe stepped to the throne, his intention to place his half of the seal into the oval. His first attempt, though, was awkward, and he struggled to make it fit. The queen harrumphed at the boy's clumsy effort. At first he was unsettled by the blunder, but as he continued to turn the piece ever so slowly, Philippe felt a quiet calm overcome him; and suddenly he understood that Caroline was right: he did truly "fale" it. He was in fact the prince! With his realization, the pendant snapped into place with a loud click. It was a perfect fit! The seal was complete!

The queen stepped back in disbelief. She knew she had sent the boy to his death. She glared at Lord Mooch; he had betrayed her for the last time!

"Long live Prince Philippe!" The crowd shouted "Long live Philippe! Long live the king! Hail to the king!"

Philippe raised his arms in salute to the people while the queen, obviously shaken, attempted to collect herself. The crowd cheered with gay abandon as they acknowledged the return of their true king!

## CHAPTER 17

# Lighten Up!

"Guard, arrest them! Take them to the dungeon!" It was Drizelda's sinister voice. "Arrest them!" the queen commanded.

"Yes arrest them!" Lord Mooch shouted "Arrest them!" For an instant, the scene was frozen in time, until the guards leaped into action, drawing their swords and forming a protective circle around the queen. Meanwhile, the guard closest to Philippe grabbed the youth, putting a dagger to his throat. In the commotion, Uni rose up on his hind quarters, his hooves thrashing.

"My God, that's what I'm talk'n about!" Jean Claude shouted as he threw one of the black guards aside.

"*Sacre bleu!*" Francois cried as he pushed and shoved, making his way toward Caroline and Philippe.

"I order you to stop this nonsense now!" It was Lord Mooch. "If you want the boy to live, you'll stop now! Stop now!" He warned again, pointing to Philippe and the guard holding the knife to Philippe's throat.

In the melee, the guards struggling to hold the great unicorn were completely and utterly astonished when the very large creature suddenly and inexplicably vanished with a poof, leaving behind just a very small quadruped with a floppy appendage stuck to his nose—singular in nature, not large, and of no apparent use or consequence.

"Not so fast, Drizelda!" Caroline warned. "You won't get away with this! Give up the throne now and you will be treated fairly!"

"That's what I'm talk'n about," Jean Claude encouraged. "My God, that's what I'm talk'n about!"

At this point, the large guardsmen holding Philippe tightened his grip on the youth and looked to Drizelda. The queen cackled a sinister laugh as she turned to reckon with the girl. "Do you think you frighten me, you upstart wench?" she snarled. "Oh my, I'm just frozen with fear, can't you tell? I think it's about time you learn your lesson!"

As Uni listened, he knew what he had to do. His new—old body—would give him the advantage he needed. He was curiously calm as he remembered that night in the forest with Burble and the troll. Meanwhile, the crowd held its collective breath.

"This is your last chance, Drizelda!" Caroline heard herself say, not knowing for sure what was going to happen next. The queen, stone-faced, hesitated for a moment before letting out a sinister cackle.

"I'm so afraid," she said, looking at Caroline with an angry stare and her voice filled with sarcasm, "so very much afraid! What are you going to do? Threaten me with your, your … unicorn?" she asked. "Look at him," she snickered. "What a pipsqueak, a stuffed toy? My, how terrifying! So incredibly frightening! So remarkably silly looking!" she snarled.

The queen, in fact, had, at this point, found the little unicorn to be so hilarious that, before she could stop herself, she let out a giggle. Completely surprised by the unexpected outburst, she clapped a hand over her mouth. But to her utter dismay, the minute she removed it, she giggled again. At first she wasn't sure but lifting her hand again, to her horror, she kept right on laughing, finding it impossible to stop. By now, it had become painfully obvious—more than obvious to the queen—that her propensity for laughter, was oddly enough, uncontrollable, leaving the normally stoic monarch, the usually deadpan patriarch, the so-often stone-faced ruler, completely and absolutely unable to stop laughing. To add to the oddity, the queen appeared to be completely captivated by the little creature with the floppy thing on his nose; she found it next to impossible to take her eyes off the funny-looking little fellow.

Now, with the crowd looking on, and much to the queen's chagrin, the misunderstood monarch kept right on laughing. To make matters worse, she couldn't seem to temper her laughter, not even a little bit. To her complete chagrin, the queen, in fact had never felt so silly.

As her reverie increased, she grabbed her tummy, giggling uncontrollably, before espousing a hardy "Ha, ha, ha!"

By now, the black guard was gawking in disbelief at their lightened-up, laughing leader, and the whole crowd appeared to have relaxed. Meanwhile, Uni found himself rather enjoying the show.

## Nothing Like a Good Laugh!

"Ha, ha, ha, ha, ha, ha!" Drizelda chortled, laughing with so much gusto now that she stumbled backward in her reverie, flopping disheveled onto the throne. By now, everyone was chuckling as laughter rippled round the room.

"I never—ha, ha, ha!—laugh!" she cried. "I hate—ha, ha!— to laugh! I can't stand—ha, ha, ha!— to laugh! I forbid—ha, ha, ha!— laughter in this—ha, ha, ha!— kingdom!" she chortled. It was becoming obvious now that the queen's incessant laughter was reaching its zenith as her beady eyes grew as large as saucers, her jaw dropping in disbelief while a hush fell over the crowd.

"What's happening to me?" she cried as she looked down at herself. "I don't know what's happening! I'm feeling so strange!"

And so it was, at this very moment, that it had become well apparent, that, by now, the queen the much maligned monarch—the queen, the formerly misguided magistrate, was oddly enough, melting, transforming as she did so into numerous teeny-weenie shimmering shards of radiant rainbow colors.

Yes, by now there was absolutely no question—yes, not even a shadow of a doubt that the queen, the formerly heavy-handed despot, the formerly taciturn tyrant, with the utmost of finality, had once and for all lightened up.

It was after this incredible transformation was completely complete and, following a brief pause during which her majesty shown exceedingly bright, that the shimmering monarch, the oh-so-radiant royal, simply and inexplicably vanished with a poof.

## Hail to the King!

"Hail King Philippe! "Hail to the king! Long live the king!" the crowd shouted. At this point, following the uncanny sequence of events, the guards sheathed their swords, kneeling to their king.

"That's what I'm talk'n about!" Jean Claude shouted

"It eez a miracle!" Francois said with a chuckle.

As the crowd cheered, Caroline spoke to Philippe, reminding him there remained a deed of great importance left for them to do.

## All You Need is Love

Ali lay motionless in the lantern; it had been days now, and she was very weak. She wasn't sure how much longer she would last. As she listened to her breath moving in and out, she sensed she would simply fall asleep one last time.

Suddenly, she heard rapid footsteps echoing in the passageway. To her surprise, the dweazel guard's expression was one of concern as he hoisted her tiny prison

## With a Little Help from Friends

Back inside the palace chamber, Lord Mooch set the princess on the throne with great care as she lay inside the tiny prison, barely breathing.

"Uni and I have traveled far to find my friend, and I am overjoyed to have found her and sad to see that she is in such a state," Caroline told the people of the court.

"Drizelda would stop at nothing; her lust for power consumed her. Drizland and its people are saved; we must now turn our energy to the princess. We must save the one who has saved this land! We must summon the magic on her behalf. We must truly believe in the magic!" With that, Caroline asked Uni to come forward as she removed the lanyard from her neck.

## If You Truly Believe

"It is my belief that it isn't the stone as much as it is the one using the stone that will bring the magic. If we have the faith, the magic will come; if we truly believe, the magic will come, and we will save Ali!"

With that, Caroline placed her hand on the stone and began rubbing in a slow, circular motion. The hall was silent as Ali lay still; her tiny form giving little hope to the concerned crowd.

Caroline rubbed the stone for what seemed like forever, but there was nothing. A tear trickled down her cheek as she stepped back, feeling defeated.

## The Blue Light of Consciousness

It was a blue spark that came first—its titillating light piercing the glaze of the stone before expanding into reds and greens and yellows, filling the hall with its shimmering light. In an instant, the hall was awash with vibrant colors. The people stood in awe, enchanted.

"It's amazing!" said one.

"The colors are fantastic!" cried another.

"Ali!" Caroline cried. "She's alive! She's alive!" The princess's eyes opened with the first spark of color. Now as she felt the life surging back into her tiny body, she sat up, and the crowd breathed a heartfelt sigh of relief.

It was Caroline who first caught the garden girl's eye, and Ali smiled at her friend. After a stretch and a yawn, looking slightly ruffled, she stepped to the door of her tiny prison and pushed it open.

## I Believe I Can Fly

In the next moment, she spread her beautiful, lace-like wings, launching herself into the air. As she rose above the crowd, the room fell silent.

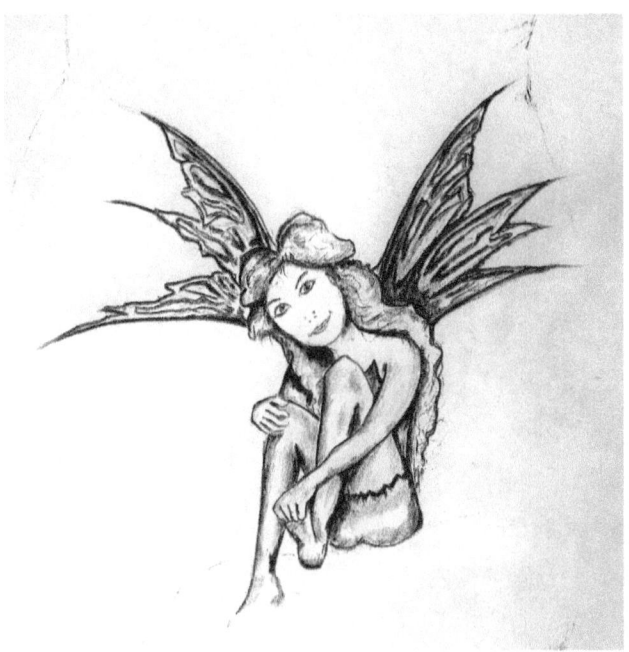

"People of Drizland," the princess spoke. "By keep'n the faith, you'de be cutt'n me tethers 'n' sett'n me free! More to the joy by keep'n the faith 'n' know'n the magic; the likes a you and yours have seen the light, as sure as day ... to the joy! You now live in a free land—a wonderland, a dreamland, the truth known."

"That's what I'm talk'n about!" Jean Claude shouted.

Philippe clasped Caroline's hand as they watched Ali rising higher and higher above the crowd. "To the joy!" Ali spoke, her voice lingering on the gentle breeze. And then, accompanied by the sound of holy chimes, she disappeared into light.

# CHAPTER 18

## *Blinded by the Light*

"Believe in the magic!" the voice spoke as Caroline shaded her eyes from the bright light "And to the joy!"

As she awakened, further shading her eyes from the morning sun that poured through the shed's crystal window, Caroline, recognizing the sound of her own voice spoke again in a gentle tone. "Believe in the magic," she said.

*I remember the flickering candle,* she thought to herself, and then there was Ali, flying above the crowd.

"To the joy," she whispered.

Caroline had been lying on her bed, staring through the shed's summer window when she heard a knock on the door.

"Caroline, are you awake?" her father asked.

"Come in, Dad," she answered.

"How are you feeling?" he asked, lowering his head and entering the room.

"Believe it or not, I think I'm good," Caroline told him. "I guess I've been pretty sick. Has it been a long time?"

"You could say that." Her father told her. "You've been delirious with a fever for a couple of days," he explained. "It was sure a relief when your fever broke," he said. "I'm glad to see you're feeling better." He shared, "Are you hungry? Would you like breakfast?"

"Sounds good; I'm kinda starving," Caroline admitted.

"That's a good sign," he told her. "I'll meet you in the kitchen when you're ready," he said, turning and heading back to the house.

"Wow, Uni—or should I call you Unis?" Caroline chuckled, holding up her little friend. We did it! We rescued Ali … sort of," she told him with a puzzled look on her face. "One thing I'm not sure I get," she told him as a tiny slipper materialized out of sight behind her on the windowsill. "I feel like Ali is fine and all," she told him. "She's just fine, she's gonna be okay, but I'm not sure—I'm really not sure—that we'll ever see her again." In that same instant, the tiny slipper dropped to the floor, shining bright for an instant before fading in the morning sun. "It's really hard to know," Caroline told him. "I sure hope we do!" In his silence, as he watched the tiny slipper disappear, Uni seemed to agree.


A Mother's Daughter


"I'm really glad you're feeling better," her father told Caroline as she sat down at the kitchen table.

"Dad," Caroline asked, turning to look at her father, "do you believe in fairies?"

"Some people do," he replied, looking at his daughter with a curious smile. "Your mother sure believed in them!" he told her. "She believed in the garden people and more."

"She did?" Caroline asked.

"She did … does," her father assured her.

"Caroline, it's important that I let you know," her father continued, " your stepmother has gone."

"She has?" Caroline said. "When will she be back?"

"She won't be coming back. Life at Morning Cloud just wasn't for her, so she went back to the city."

"Oh?" Caroline said, trying not to look excited.

"I want you to know there's enough money for you to go to school in the city."

"Thanks, Dad," Caroline told him. "There'll never be any place like Morning Cloud." She said, "Dad, I have a question for you: what was that tune you were humming when I walked into the kitchen?"

"Oh, I don't know, just a song from a long time ago. It's an old song sung by a father to his young daughter," he explained. "He's awestruck by the miracle of her new life."

"Before she was born, he was forlorn?" Caroline inquired.

"How would you know that?" her father asked, looking at his daughter out of the corner of his eye.

"Oh, I don't know, a dream, an ancient memory ... I'm not sure—really not sure," she said, looking at her father with an impish grin.

"I can't believe you would remember that song!" he said.

"It's been a long time since I've ... ah, I mean, since your little friend has sung it; a long time since before your mother died," he told her. "When your mother got sick, I'm afraid the music nearly died with her. It's taken too long for me to get over losing her," he confessed. "I didn't realize, until it was almost too late, how lucky I am to have you!"

"I had a dream, Dad," Caroline told him.

"Oh?" he said eyeing his daughter.

"Mom was there, and you were there, and you were singing; it was nice."

"Oh," her father said quietly, pretending to rub a speck of dust from his eye. "How about some breakfast?" he asked

"Great! I'm starving!" Caroline spoke, "Dad."

"Yes," he replied, looking at his daughter as though he hadn't seen her in a long time.

"I love your song!"

"I can't believe you remember. Perhaps your friend will sing it for you sometime. It's amazing you still have the little fellow after all these years!"

"He's been with me through thick and thin," she said. "It seems like he'll be around forever. I really think he's got the magic."

"You sound just like your mother," her dad said with a chuckle. "I have to say, there is something special about that little fellow."

"I'm sure of it!" Caroline agreed.

"Enjoy your breakfast," her father encouraged as he looked through the kitchen door into the summer's day.

"It's a beautiful morning," he observed. "It's already getting warm."

# *A Familiar Young Man*

Caroline jumped when a young man appeared unexpectedly at the open kitchen door.

"*Bonjour*, Monsieur Fairchild!" the youth said with a smile. He was a handsome young man with blue eyes and curly brown hair.

"Ah, there you are, Philippe!" her father replied. "Bonjour, good morning. Caroline, this is Philippe," her father told her, introducing his startled daughter. "Philippe is here to help Jean-Claude and I with the lavender harvest."

"Hello, Caroline sputtered, nearly choking on her juice.

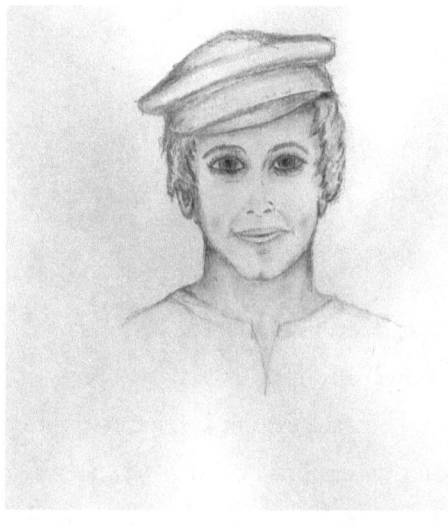

"Are you okay, sweetheart?"

"I'm fine, Dad," Caroline told him, feeling a bit embarrassed.

"*Hallo*, Caroline," Philippe said. "I've heard so much about you, I feel like I know you. I'm so glad to see you're feeling better."

"You seem familiar to me as well," Caroline told him with a wry grin.

"Did you ride the Black, Philippe?" her father asked.

"He's just outside on the hitching post, Monsieur Fairchild," Philippe told him.

"What a pretty pendant," Caroline observed as she studied the stone hanging from Philippe's neck.

"It was a gift," he replied. "It's called a—"

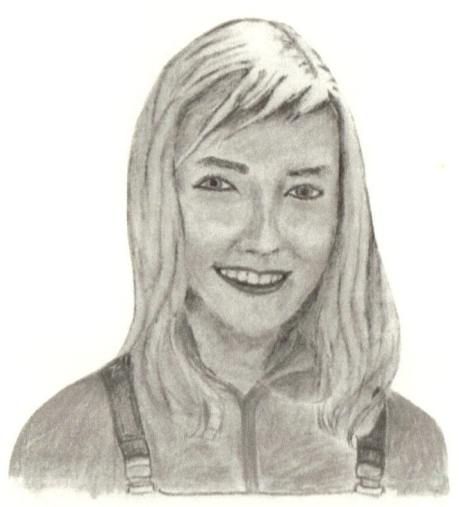

"A Rainbow Stone," Caroline offered.

"How did you know?" Philippe asked.

As Caroline looked beyond Philippe into the summer's day, she spied a rainbow drifting on the remains of the misty morning.

"I'm not sure," she said with a smile. "A dream, perhaps … or just an ancient memory from long ago."

As she looked into Philippe's eyes, in the magic of the moment, it appeared to Caroline as if the rainbow had come to rest on the young man's shoulders. In his silence, Uni seemed to agree.

The End

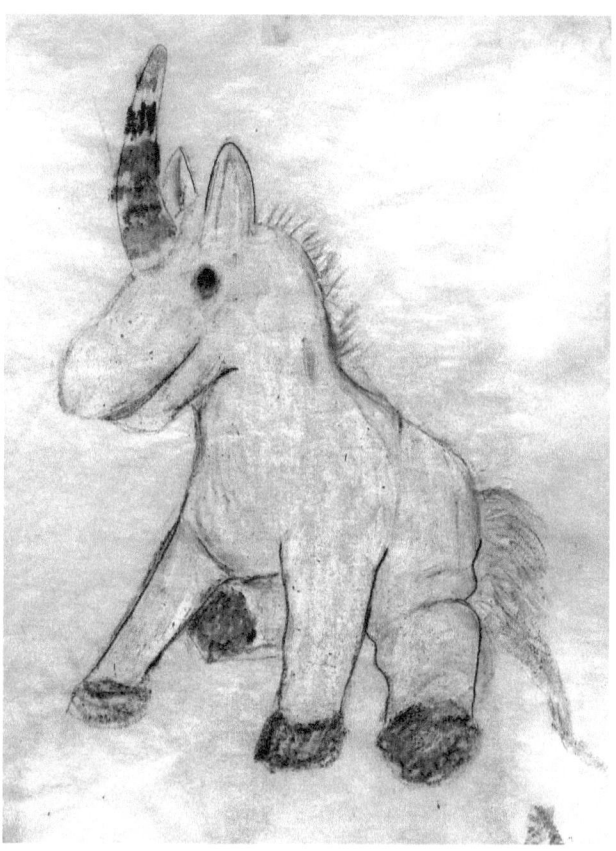

# AFTERWORD

And so Caroline rescued Ali—or perhaps, as the Shadow Master suggested, it was Ali who rescued Caroline—and in doing so, learned a few things about herself. She learned to face her fear and let it go, to acknowledge her doubt and accept it for what it was—just that, and to understand that mistakes are ultimately opportunities from which to learn. Perhaps most importantly, she learned to trust herself and follow her heart.

Her friend Uni discovered that which he already knew, but according to Burble, didn't remember that he knew: "All ya need is love," because, like Ali tried to explain, all we really ever have is love, not tomorrow's or yesterday's, but today's, right now.

I guess each of us has our own Forest of Shadows, but like the Shadow Master said, "Without the light there can be no shadows." The shadows aren't real, so the Shadow Master claims; easy for him to say but somehow deep down I think I'm beginning to understand.

Fortunately for Drizland, Mimi was nosey enough to know about Philippe and the pendant and savvy enough to tell Caroline about it. I'm not sure just how that little piece of royal crest would have made it back into place otherwise.

Perhaps the most interesting twist to this tale came to light years later, when the story was being retold by an old innkeeper by the name of Francois.

According to legend, good King Philippe was very wise, and when he realized his time was running short, he spoke to his queen, telling her that he feared for the future of the kingdom and its young prince. There were dark forces at work, sinister in nature; the land and its people were in danger, and, without guidance, he feared the worst for the future of the kingdom.

It was then that the good king, in his wisdom, asked his queen to hide the young prince and to take on the roll of the dark queen. The king knew that it would be the only way to save the kingdom. Because of the queen's great love for her king, she had no choice but to accept.

It was in the end when the queen experienced the magic of the little unicorn that she realized that she had attained her final state and was overcome with joy. To her delight, as she sat staring at Uni, the giggling monarch suddenly understood: her destiny had been fulfilled, and her duty finished. In the spirit of a true thespian, and, to the glory, she had played the roll of the dark queen to perfection.

And so, beginning with a young girl's tragic loss and ending with a fairy princess flying to the light; Prince Philippe was saved, the kingdom was safe, and the dreamland was restored to the grandeur it had once known. All's well that ends well.

As for the Rainbow Stone, it's been said the stone is as real as you make it—like a stone in your shoe or a pebble you might find on the beach. Be that as it may, should you one day be so lucky as to find a small, round, silky-smooth stone appearing to shine of its own accord, give it a rub and … to the joy!

SGMKJ

# About the Author

Dr. Bob Ward lives with his wife, Cindy, and their numerous animals on their small hobby farm on Vashon Island, in Puget Sound in Washington State. He is a family dentist, a teacher at the University of Washington, and a mentor to several continuing education study groups in the United States and Europe. While he has done extensive writings in the professional ranks, his jump to fiction and children's stories has been relatively recent.

*Le Rêve (The Dream)*, a story inspired by the relationship between his young daughter and her little unicorn friend, existed as an idea for over twenty years before finally being written down. "When she was young," he writes, "my daughter was given the gift of a little stuffed animal. He was a well-mannered critter, and it wasn't long before the three of us were fast friends." He goes on to say, "While I'm sure many parents have communicated with their kids by talking to them with toys, I couldn't have imagined how much fun it would be pretending to be the voice of that fuzzy little fellow." And so the story began ...

An avid reader of myths, legends and just plain tall tales, Dr. Bob couldn't help but draw inspiration from several classic works while creating *Le Rêve*. The rescue of the feminine is archetypal in nature, he explains, and has occurred from ancient myths to modern-day tales. In the Hindu epic, The Ramayana, Sita is taken to Sri Lanka; in the Greek myth, Helen is taken to Troy; and in the modern classic, Beauty is held captive by the Beast.

He finishes by saying that he is inclined to believe his yarn, his tale, is both fairy tale and myth. Joseph Campbell says the two are kindred. If Mr. Campbell says myths are songs of the universe, Dr. Bob would hope that this tale might just be ... a simple melody.

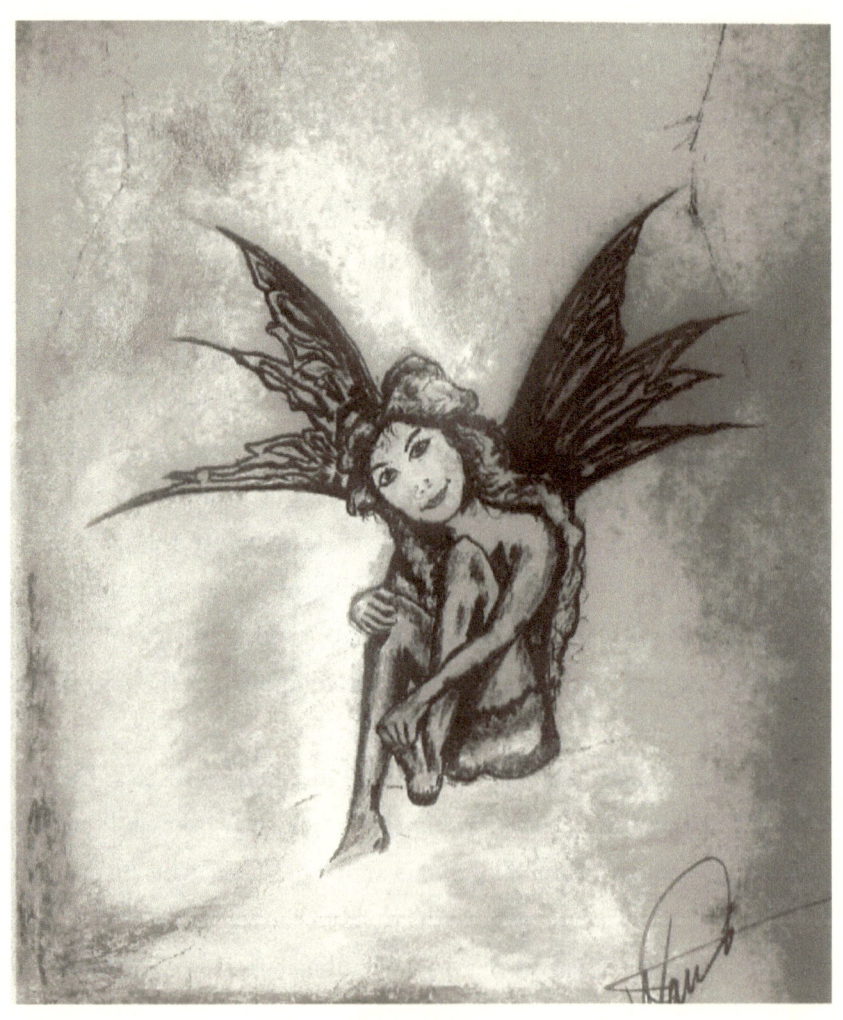

To the Joy